PORTRAIT OF A FAMILY, THE GLADSTONES 1839-1889

By Penelope Gladstone

Illustrations by Pat Smith

British Library Cataloguing in Publication Data
Gladstone, Penelope Anne, *1930-*
Portrait of a family: the Gladstones, 1839-1889-
  1. Great Britain. Gladstone, W. E. (William Ewart),
  1809-1889 — Biographies
  941.081'092'4

ISBN 1-871482-02-X

Distributed by Thomas Lyster Ltd., 48, Southport Road,
Ormskirk, Lancashire L39 1QR.
Telephone: Ormskirk (0695) 75112.
Fax: Ormskirk (0695) 70120.

Printed in England by Titus Wilson & Son Ltd, Kendal.

Acknowledgements

My thanks are due to those who run the Newspaper Library of the British Museum at Colindale so excellently, without which this book could never have been written; also to the Department of Manuscripts and Department of Printed Books of the British Museum. The London Library has been my main source for books written during the Victorian period and by those who lived to know it first hand, and to their staff and those of the numerous public libraries I have used, especially the City of Westminster public libraries, I am deeply appreciative. I owe much to the Clwyd Record Office; also I would like to thank the National Library of Wales, the Essex Record Office, the Leeds District Archives, and the Grange Museum of Local History at Neasden. I would like to thank Osyth Leeston for her suggestion of using as much variety as possible in the stories I selected to tell, and Georgina Battiscombe, author of the delightful biography *Mrs. Gladstone* (1956), for her time and valuable help.

Finally, I give grateful thanks to my family and cousins for their encouragement in this enjoyable task, and especially my brother William for editing the book with the minimum of corrections and the maximum of tact, and to Pat Smith for her care with the delightful illustrations.

Contents

Introduction

Contrary to what many people presume Queen Victoria was friendly with William and Catherine Gladstone for the first thirty-five years of their married life, until the politics of the Eastern Question intervened. This book reveals the lives of the politician's eight children and his devoted wife, so totally different a personality to himself. Their children were by coincidence of the same age as the royal family, and the Prince of Wales, Princess Louise, and Prince Leopold became especial friends.

To make it easy to read the book is arranged in a series of stories covering many and varied events, from episodes of family life to how they responded to adventures that caused excitement and anxiety at the time. The children, their schools, their home and cousins are described; what their mother did in her spare time is disclosed, as are their favourite servants, the secretaries, and those gentlemen who firmly attached themselves who were referred to as Mr. Gladstone's attendant satellites.

They lived mainly in London, but were frequently away either with friends or electioneering, and almost every year there were travels abroad for recreation and a change. The boys often went off in pairs to where they chose, Iceland, the Channel Islands, Madeira, and climbing in Switzerland before the rush of tourists; the parents usually with two of their children to Germany and Italy. In later life they would go on a cruise, an invitation extended no doubt to make such a recreation fashionable, and once explored the Norwegian fiords on the *Sunbeam*, the private yacht whose voyage round the world has recently been reprinted.

How fascinating to explore the thoughts behind the customs and conventions

that surrounded them, and what a delight the book has been to work on, discovering which year an old letter was written, and why it mentioned curious details a member of the family felt should be kept as a momento to reflect some unique event that caused perhaps amusement, perhaps panic, at the time. It has led me to delve into many papers and to browse through masses of old newspapers and what I have discovered was news to me. Indeed, so far as I know these stories will be new to the reader, though many were spoken of when they took place. Other happenings which were private had to be hushed up and kept quiet, as the reader will realise. All these family occasions, many charged with emotion, might have been forgotten for ever but for a conversation that took place in 1982 between Dossie Parish, my father's first cousin, and myself.

'Oh, didn't you know I went to see Queen Victoria,' she told me, 'I suppose it was really because she wanted to hear about my grandparents.'

It was in 1897 that the six-year old Dossie went to see the elderly Queen at Windsor Castle. The little girl, remarkable for her extraordinarily thick hair of ringlets, and her mother, Mary Drew, spent the previous night at Kensington Palace, at the invitation of Princess Louise, Marchioness of Lorne, who had written:-

Dear Mary,
. . . The Queen just lets me know she would like to see you on Thursday next. Will you therefore come here the evening before, and we will then go down together. I hope this will suit you. I am sure there must be some convenient train or other which would bring you here in time for Dorothy to have a good tea before going to bed. . .
    In haste,
      Yours sincerely,
        Louise[1]

After the good tea and one hopes a good night, for Princess Louise in her pretty blue dressing-gown with blue ribbons hanging down had kissed Dossie goodnight; the little girl, her mother and the Princess took the train to Windsor the next day. They then got into a shining carriage drawn by two elegant white horses, and as they drove up the steep hill to the Castle Dossie noticed a mounted groom rode between them and the pavement. The carriage entered the gate and as soon as it drew to a halt she jumped out and ran into the doorway. There, coming towards her, was a lady in black. Dossie had not expected to see the Queen so soon, but she remembered what she had been told and curtsied deeply, but then her mother caught up with her and greeted the lady as Princess Beatrice!

It was by then two o'clock and Dossie and her mother found themselves invited to lunch with the Queen's household. The little girl, aware of her small size, felt determined to overcome her shyness as she explained she had come to see the Queen, and a kindly lady asked her if she had ever seen the Queen before? Well, she had seen the Queen sitting in her carriage, so she made a pertinent reply, unaware of the mirth it would cause:-

'Yes, I have seen the Queen. But she hasn't seen me.'

After lunch the visitors were shown into their sitting rooms. Dossie noticed a nice fire burning merrily in hers; a piano — in case one wanted to play the piano — and a bed, made up just as if one was going to stay the night. She changed into her white silk dress with yellow sash that had been bought from Liberty's and her new silk gloves.

Princess Louise told mother and I to take off our right hand glove. We walked along the long, long corridor and at the end was an Indian man who the Queen likes very much. The Queen was sitting down in a chair with a white cap on.[2]

Dossie directly walked towards the Queen and standing by the footstool leant forward to give a kiss. At the same time the Queen's outstretched arms drew the child towards her so that the child lost her balance. After they had extricated themselves, the Queen asked the little girl her name.

'Dorothy.'

'But what are you called?'

'Dossie.'

'How old are you?'

Mary Drew promptly answered, 'Seven.' Was she hoping to please Her Majesty by adding another year?

'What do you call your grandfather?'

'Papa.'

'Then what do you call your father?'

'Father,' was the sensible reply.

'And your grandmother?' queried Her Majesty.

'Dan-dan.'

Dossie was then instructed to move so that she was standing against the light, and the Queen slowly pulled on her spectacles to examine the child in profile. A little box with a brooch was then presented, and Dossie did what she had been told to do. She kissed the Queen's hand and gave another curtsey. After this her concentration wandered for she was watching the Munshi, who waited behind the Queen's chair dressed in brilliant colours with a cluster of jewels pinned to his turban. The Munshi was an Indian Mohammedan whom the Queen had engaged after the death of her Scottish groom and friend, John Brown. He was invariably at Her Majesty's beck and call, and when she signed papers he knew precisely how long to wait until the ink was dry. As Dossie stared in wonderment at the splendidly attired Munshi standing motionless, her mother and the Queen talked, as Dossie later recorded, about a lot of things.

Afterwards when they had said goodbye, kissed and curtseyed again, they had to wait for Princess Louise, who was going to the station with them, whilst out of the window they glimpsed the Queen going out in her carriage with outriders. Arriving at Windsor station Dossie was surprised to hear that the train had been kept waiting specially for them.

In old prints and photographs Dossie is often to be seen with her illustrious grandparents, William and Catherine Gladstone. In old age they adored having the little girl with them, and when they went out in the Victoria, the carriage with the big folded-back hood which took only two passengers, there was a little bench opposite where Dossie could sit. As she remembered how she had to balance holding on with both hands, other childhood memories flooded back, a link for me with the past, for the Gladstones had a family of eight children, but we will first turn the clock back to the day they were married.

1

The Double Wedding

When Catherine became engaged to William Gladstone and Mary to George Lyttelton within a short space of time, plans were made for them both to be married on the same day. The sisters were close in age and close in affection. Since their father was no longer alive Catherine was given in marriage by Stephen, and Mary by Henry. Stephen and Henry Glynne were Catherine's and Mary's elder brothers. At Hawarden Stephen was the squire and Henry was the Rector.

Hawarden is a village on the edge of the Welsh hills lying six miles west from Chester, and on July 29th 1839 it was decorated with arches of laurel with flags and flowers and ribbons. From early morning the main street, called the Highway because it was on the route from Chester to Holyhead, became alive with pedestrians, horsemen, chariots, carriages, gigs, and farm carts bringing on-lookers. To announce the wedding the church bells rang out. Then a slow moving procession made its way towards the church led by various bands dressed in bright colours and carrying their banners. The *Chester Courant* described the sequence through the village:-

> The procession was then formed led by the the Odd Fellows preceded by their band; then a group from the temperance societies, and another group of people from the benefit societies, each led by a band. A fourth band led a large number of local tradesmen.
> The brides and bridegrooms, relations and guests followed in twelve carriages of various sorts. The fifth held the brides and their two brothers, the sixth and seventh the bridegrooms; these carriages being drawn by four horses, accompanied by postilions Finally, came Lady Glynne's pony carriage holding Mrs. Hand, the housekeeper, and Mr. Whittingham, the butler, whom had been with the family for over forty years.

The brides were married by their Uncle George, the Reverend and Honourable George Neville Grenville, who had previously been rector of the parish and then became Dean of Windsor and, at the same time, Master of Magdalen College, Cambridge. Ample in size, he had a loud laugh and a very large family. Three of his daughters were bridesmaids; also William's younger sister, Helen, and two other friends. The two brides were dressed identically in white satin with a peach tint, trimmed with lavish flounces of Brussels lace.[1] On their heads they wore orange blossom wreaths bearing a diamond brooch in the centre. The bridesmaids were more modestly dressed in muslin with pale pink trimmings, and crape and lace bonnets with wreaths of orange blossom similar to the brides.

Following the ceremony there was a reception for the bridal party and close friends, described as 'an elegant déjeuner,' in the *Chester Courant*. There were further celebrations in the village inn where a three o'clock dinner, 'a very good and substantial one,' was served at the Glynne Arms. Afterwards several toasts were drunk, first to the Queen and the royal family. Then the glasses were refilled to drink to the health of the newly-married couples. With a Welsh lilt to his voice the Chairman of the proceedings announced:-

The health of Mr. and Mrs. Gladstone, and with luck and a lad!'
    Then he called for three cheers, but not only three but three times three and one cheer more.
    The Chairman then said, he was sure they would feel the greatest anxiety until they had drunk the next toast, and he would therefore neither deprive himself or the company any longer of the pleasure they would receive from so doing. He proposed most heartily 'The healths of Lord and Lady Lyttelton,' with the same accompaniment as before — 'luck and a lad!' then three times three and one cheer more.

Meanwhile, the two couples departed: William and Catherine Gladstone to Norton Priory, a fine house they had been lent in Cheshire; and George and Mary Lyttelton to Hagley Hall, near Birmingham, the family seat of the Lytteltons. George Lyttelton's widowed mother, Sarah, Lady Lyttelton, had had to stay at Hagley Hall to look after his two sisters, Caroline and Lavinia, who had the measles. William's father had come from Scotland (his mother was no longer alive) with his two eldest brothers, Thomas and Robertson, who had both attended bringing their wives and their carriages. The brides' mother, Lady Glynne, who had become increasingly solitary since the death of her husband and had delicate health, secluded herself away from the wedding. But the festivities in the village continued late with a dance held in a nearby field, 'a well selected spot' as the dancers had not far to go to the pub, with a band on a large platform. Finally there was a display of fireworks. Afterwards money and new clothes were distributed to the poor and to those unable to attend.

William Gladstone had got to know Stephen Glynne when they were both undergraduates at Oxford, and had attended the same college, Christ Church. Catherine found her husband was as different from her brothers as could be, the very opposite in personality. Whereas William always wanted to lead and was ambitious, Stephen and Henry were modest and never sought attention. They had been brought up at Hawarden where they remained to live as squire and Rector. They became known in the locality as 'the gentle brethren,' a nickname that suited them exactly. They were neither tall nor short, nor particularly noticeable in any way though of distinguished heritage. Yet their sympathetic smiles and voices made them easily approachable and they mixed equally well with villagers and gentry, for conversation with them came easily. Catherine and Mary were more lively and forceful than their brothers, with Catherine, a couple of years older than Mary, usually taking the lead. Three years after the wedding of 1839 Henry Glynne married Lavinia Lyttelton; Stephen remained a bachelor.

The Glynnes, as many Victorian families were apt to do, created a language to suit themselves, and especially Catherine invented her own vocabulary for a person or a feeling, and had been given every encouragement by her brothers who would add further suggestions, as they heard the sisters laughing together. When George Lyttelton heard this family language he called it Glynnese, and compiled enough words to make up a little book, which he called *A Glossary of the Glynne Language*[2]

One remark that was unique to Glynnese was 'bathing feel.' This described anticipation of an event when one was nervous yet excited. Catherine delighted in being excited; Mary too, but not so much. As youngsters they went with their brothers to the sea to the North Wales coast, where the water was apt to be chilly for swimming. The children were terrified of being pulled in from a bathing machine. The bathing machine consisted of a horse-drawn covered cart in which they would change into their voluminous swimwear. When the horse pulled the cart into the sea the door at the side would open and at the bottom of some steps a robust woman pulled the shivering children into the icy-feeling water with her pink muscular arms. The very thought was enough to send shivers down the spine for the rest of their lives.

A person they liked, or felt comfortable with even if they had little in common, was referred to as 'an old shoe.' An old shoe was a person one felt familiar with and who did not cramp one's style. They both felt sorting out their drawers and desks was a tedious task. As they received letters which accumulated so they had to make space on their writing desks to write replies. Then came the decision of what to throw away and what they still wanted to keep. Rubbish they threw away they called 'groutle' and rubbish they kept they called 'hydra.' The difference between groutle and hydra depended on the mood of the owner, and the exact definition of these words was very sensibly never arrived at.

Catherine and Mary were also apt to use remarks such as 'I could have died' when something amused them; and 'unearthly' when a thrilling vision met their eyes. To 'troll' was to chat, or write a newsy letter; and a 'break' meant a break from routine, and always indicated an event or friend to be looked forward to. A 'break plus' meant a special event or meeting. They remained as very close sisters, and as their families grew the children became a united happy crowd.

Catherine eventually had eight children and Mary had twelve. At Catherine's first confinement her two aunts, Lady Wenlock and Lady Braybrooke, stayed with her encouraging her to 'cry out.' A midwife was always called to attend the births, and it seems that William was there if he could be. At other times he had gone to fetch Dr. Locock, who was small and slight and had such an understanding manner that his patients placed implicit confidence in him. He was the obstetrician for all the Gladstone and Lyttelton babies, and attended the Queen for her nine, and was sought after by all fashionable London.

As the Gladstone children arrived nurses and governesses joined the family, and both parents gave lessons. When the day came for the eldest to go off to boarding school, not only Willy but William too, was suffering from 'bathing feel.'

2

Geddington and Eton

In January 1850 Willy was taken by his father to his first boarding school. He was dressed in a peaked cap, short jacket and loose trousers. His father wore a top hat and carried his son's portmanteau. Father and son strongly resembled each other in looks, having plentiful dark curly hair and penetrating dark eyes. They had parted from the rest of the family at Birmingham and Willy, the eldest aged nine, had burst into tears at leaving Mama, his brother and four sisters. Willy and his father took the train to Northampton; they chatted happily together. They spent the night at an inn and the next morning caught the seven o'clock train to Wellingborough, where they enjoyed a good breakfast. From there it was necessary to hire a cab for the last ten miles to Geddington, a village just north of Kettering. They talked of the beauty of the Northamptonshire countryside, though as father and son were very close to each other they were preoccupied with the thought of parting.

The ancient village of Geddington was dominated by a magnificent Norman church, in front of which stood an exquisite monument, an Eleanor Cross, similar to the one at Charing Cross in London, but better preserved. The cab passed through the village to reach the new vicarage which had just been completed to accommodate the boys who were tutored by the Vicar, whose name was appropriately Mr. Church. It was a fine Victorian gothic building set back from the road. The pointed windows had trellis grill ironwork which cut out much of the light and made for an austere atmosphere.

The new boy and his father were greeted by Mr. and Mrs. Church and shown round the school at leisure, and after four hours it was time to part. The heavy front door clanged shut, and tearful Willy was left feeling homesick and lost, whilst on the other side of the door his father, after the last embrace and farewell, felt even worse as he left on his way to London.[1]

The school had been established for his own sons by the Duke of Buccleuch, whose magnificent palace Boughton, built in the style of Versailles, was a mile away. The Duke, as patron of the living, had appointed Mr. Church as Vicar but to run the school, most of the parish work being left to the curate. A few of the Duke's friends and acquaintances were invited to send their sons there. Willy achieved this privilege because his grandfather and the Duke had been partners in certain Scottish ventures, including the Burntisland Ferry, an early steamship crossing the Firth of Forth.

The new vicarage had been specially built for the boys, who slept in a bleak dormitory on the top floor. Willy wrote to his father as soon as he could, and that was the next day:-

My darling Papa,
    . . . Our manners are thus we get up in the morning at half past 6 and then put our boots and our socks on and then our trousers, leaving our nighshirts on and stand against the bed and say the Apostles Creed and then we kneel down and say our prayers. We begin our Latin at 7, and Mr. Church comes in and we ought to have our Latin done by that time ready to say to him . . .
    I ever remain you dear affectionate and dutiful son,
        Willy[2].

A week later he wrote:-

My darling dear Papa and Mamma,
    . . . Today when I had finished my lessons for the morning I happened to put my elbow on the table and on feeling my head it was quite wet from having tried so hard to master my Latin Exercise but I am happy to say that I did *conquer it* and oh was so happy when I had done it. It is thus that by perseverance I conquer difficulties and temptations . . .
    I remain your affec. and dutiful son,
        Willy.

No wonder Willy was missing his family. The six children with their parents had been staying with their grandfather, Sir John Gladstone, in his large country seat, Fasque, forty miles from Aberdeen. They had been there from the previous October, and the long visit had culminated with the joys of Christmas. More recently there had been snow, and adults and children had played together at making a snow house in front of the vast house of pinky-brown sandstone, that looked so well in the sun and the snow.

At Fasque his father had celebrated his fortieth birthday, which seemed a great age to Willy, who had written him a letter. In it he confided to tell the innermost secrets of his heart to his dearest Papa that he had fears that he might die soon. In point of fact his father would live to be eighty-nine and Willy would predecease him, dying from a brain tumour at the age of fifty. This was the birthday letter:-

My dearest Papa,
    It would be impossible for me to express my feelings of joy and gratitude to you; of joy because God Almighty has permitted you to come to your 40th year, but perhaps it will be your last in this life, for we know not what time the Lord cometh, and of gratitude because you will and have taught me what is necessary in knowledge, geography, Latin, and other useful things that a Christian child ought to know. Morning and evening I pray that Our Lord may send his Grace upon you, and that until your death you may fight against the wicked one and the cares of the world like a good soldier . . . .
    The Father, Son and Holy Ghost be with you and among all your relations and friends that at the last you may come to his everlasting Kingdom.
    Amen.

I write this letter instead of a present but I know you will accept this as if it was one, but it is more than a present because now I tell the most innermost secrets of my heart, but I wish that I could tell you more.

I am, dear father, your affec. grateful, happy and dutiful son,
    Willy.

Of course many children, when they hear adults talking of death, fear for the death of their parents, yet it seems more than a coincidence that Willy had this premonition. He must have realised that grandpapa was eighty-five and was nearing the end of his life. Several of his cousins had died as infants or small children leaving sorrowful gaps. Grandpapa had been visibly upset when they had left Fasque after three and half months for he knew the spacious house would seem lonely without the family, who were an enchanting and lively lot. First, there was Willy who was nine; then Agnes, prim and dainty who was seven; Stephy, pale and tall and five; and Jessy, rosy cheeked and round limbed at four; Mary, who they called Maizie, was just beginning to talk at two, and finally Lena who was still only five months old. Lena's proper name was Helen, but having chosen for their children so many names already in the family, they realised each one must have his or her own derivative of that name.

William and Catherine were woken at a quarter to four and left the house at a quarter to five. They travelled with their six children by carriage to Carlisle. A ladies maid, a children's nurse and Miss Prisk, the governess, accompanied them. We can imagine Willy sitting between the coachman and his father, well wrapped up in scarf and gloves, sharing a big rug over their legs. Inside the carriage Catherine, and her three adult helpers and the five children sat packed together with the little ones sitting on their knees. At Carlisle they spent the night in the Bush Hotel. Then the family party of eleven, filling a second-class compartment, took the train to Birmingham.

After parting from her husband and Willy, Catherine went with the other five children to stay with her sister, travelling the last twelve miles by carriage to Hagley Hall.

Hagley Hall, the home of the Lytteltons, was an imposing Palladian house, built of grey stone with large pillars each side of the entrance. Here the children were delighted to mix together; the little ones playing in the nursery. In ten and a half years of marriage Catherine had given birth to six children, and Mary to seven children and was expecting another. The elder Lyttelton children, Meriel, Lucy and Charles, did lessons with their governess, Miss Window, whilst Agnes and Stephy did their lessons with Miss Prisk. When Willy wrote letters from school to his mother, he not only had to send messages to his own brother and four sisters, but also to his seven cousins. He felt he must send them each an individual message, but as he listed the children in order of age the communications became briefer and briefer, until he simply sent his love to the babies!

Some of the Lytteltons had suffered from whooping cough and Catherine was glad none of her children had caught it, though there had been little illnesses and discomforts to worry her, as there always will be with children. Jessy, who had been christened Catherine Jessica but was known as Jessy to distinguish her from her mother, had been pained by broken chilblains on her feet. Later Catherine was to remind herself of the compliment Jessy had paid her:-

> At Hagley when so unwell and it hurt her so to walk how would she follow me, sweet lamb, to my bedroom, and sit happily in the armchair, living as it were upon a word or a look of mine. One of those days at Hagley when very poorly, I hear her sweet voice saying, 'Dear sweet Mammy, you look so kind at me'.[3]

After a month the family returned to their home at 13, Carlton Gardens, west of Trafalgar Square and within easy walking distance of the House of Commons. The house had large rooms, and in the drawing room there was a fireplace with a big mantelpiece above it. William would place Stephy and Jessy, one each end and the tiny children would try and stand motionless pretending to be ornaments. Although Jessy was a year younger than Stephy, she loved the game best and seemed quite fearless. She had a round plump face and, like her mother, highly-coloured cheeks and a mouth that easily broke into a smile, but she could be sensitive and have her moods. Someone likened her to a dormouse! Her father commented:-

> Her nurses and governesses who had begun to give her her first lessons loved her dearly and found her most docile, but anything in the nature of command given with briskness, or anything that the least looked like anger, seemed entirely to bewilder her and take away the power either of obeying or of recovering herself.
> . . . When therefore Jessy hesitated and lingered instead of doing something she was bid to do, we used to say, taking her aside for the moment, 'Now, love me, Jessy, put your arms round my neck,' and it was always answered. She would sometimes put both in a moment; sometimes more slowly, first one and then the other.

They had returned to London at the beginning of March, and on April 5th Jessy was taken ill. It was Good Friday. Dr. Locock was called, and prescribed Dover's powders, calomil and, at one stage, blistering. When Jessy could drink he recommended milk and beef tea, but the child suffered more and more from convulsions, frequently screaming aloud and keeping the household awake as her parents held her in turn. Meningitis was diagnosed. Dr. Locock visited every day and was fetched by William at night when the child would not quieten.

Jessy died ten days after Good Friday. William took the little coffin up to his father's home at Fasque. On leaving he asked Hampton, the butler, to thank the household for being so helpful. Hampton broke down and wept. When William eventually reached Fasque and met the butler there, 'Hayman wept uncontrollably and passionately as a child.'

A note written by Willy awaited the sad father when he returned to London:-

Miss Jessy Gladstone departed this life on Monday night, 1st Sunday after Easter in the year 1850. So sweetly did she sleep, so sweetly did she breathe that we most firmly hope that her spirit has been borne away by the Holy Angels to Heaven, there to enjoy perpetual rest and felicity with him who called her away from this world to himself for evermore.[4]

Willy found it hard to get over Jessy's death. The following year he was not well and developed an abscess on his neck, but there was one small compensation; Mr. Church showed his sympathy by giving Willy a glass of porter, bitter beer, with his dinner. The headmaster explained the reason for this to his father:-

Dear Sir,
   The medical man has just been here and gives an improved account of Willy . . . I find that he has set himself a Lent Rule of going without butter at breakfast and tea on Wednesday and Friday. I do not like to discourage this, and therefore have given him porter at his dinner, so that his constitution may be fully compensated.
      Believe me, dear Sir,
         Your faithful servant,
            W. W. H. Church.[5]

Willy went to Eton College when he was eleven and a half, and Stephy soon followed him from Geddington. The boys shared a bedroom with rural views over fields and enjoyed watching the trains puffing by. Stephy, who wore glasses, always suffered from poor eyesight and had to get his work done by daylight, while Willy did much of his by candle-light. The boys, whose chief delight was football, seem to have been very independent but hid little from their parents. Stephy wrote:-

There has been a fair going on at Windsor, which of course is forbidden, but I think nearly all the school got to it. It chiefly consists of lotteries and gambling places: but there is a menagerie, which is I believe the best in England, which the Queen visited.[6]

The year at Eton was divided into two halves with summer holidays and Easter holidays. In the summer holidays of 1857 Willy was invited to go on a tour organized for the Prince of Wales to Königswinter in Germany. He had been the previous summer with the Prince and three other Etonians on a walking tour in Dorset, when Königswinter had been mentioned. Willy heard that the holiday was on from the other Etonians: Wood, Cadogan and Stanley, all sons of peers. His father had known all along, but thought a fortnight's notice was enough. Willy wanted to go and was excited at the prospect, but realised that he would miss seeing his family as the tour was to last three months. He wrote:-

It has been a very engrossing subject in my thoughts for the last three weeks but at the same time I did not look upon it as certain from your long silence. I hope however I have got no harm from hearing about it from anyone before you, as I assure you I have always looked at it in a serious as well as a novel and in some respects a pleasant light. For I must say it goes *very hard indeed* with me to have no quiet recess among parents, brothers and sisters, and all dear persons and places, between two long and busy halves. On the other hand I cannot help feeling highly gratified at being privileged like this, not that the sort of thing was entirely unexpected. For just before we came home for the Easter holidays I had a sort of hint that something of this sort might turn up, and I had still slightly clung to the hope. If you remember at dinner once at home talking about secrets I said I had one keeping from you at that time, and that was it.[7]

In the middle of July Prince Albert Edward, Willy and the three Etonians left for Cologne, accompanied by as many adults. Colonel Henry Ponsonby, General Grey, Mr. F. W. Gibbs, Dr. Armstrong and Bishop Tower went with them, who were respectively, the Queen's private secretary, Prince Albert's private secretary, Prince Albert Edward's tutor, a doctor and a bishop. The boys, aged fifteen to seventeen, were all dressed alike for the holiday; the gentlemen, in what they felt to be suitable leisure wear, were all dressed differently. They settled down at Königswinter, a charming summer resort on the Rhine between Cologne and Bonn where photographs of the group were taken, the boys wearing shiny German caps with tassels.

The boys were high spirited and the adults were happy to come down to the boys' sense of humour, including Mr. Gibbs, the strict tutor the Prince Consort had chosen for his son. There were walks in the forests and hills, and a visit to Prince Metternich who was eighty-four and had retired to his castle at Johannisberg on the Rhine. They went to Coburg and visited Duke Ernst of Sax-Coburg-Gotha, elder brother of Prince Albert, at the beautiful little castle of Rosenau, where the brothers had been brought up. They then spent some time in Switzerland, where Willy in the future would return to so frequently for mountaineering; and France, and afterwards the Prince always preferred French taste to German. In October they returned to England.

A year later Willy went to Oxford University, and two years later the Prince of Wales also went to study at Oxford. Willy boarded at his college, Christ Church, and the Prince let it be known he wished he could do the same. The heir to the throne, who had had so many reservations made on his young life, was not allowed to play football or cricket. Tennis was considered suitable and Willy was considered a suitable opponent, and the two were often to be seen playing the game that had become the latest rage, lawn tennis.

3
Children's Dances

In May 1855 Catherine took her two eldest, Willy and Agnes, to a children's ball at Buckingham Palace. She also took her niece, Lucy Lyttelton. Lucy was far from shy, though she admitted 'on the way a bathing feel for nearly the first time assailed me.' Lucy was thirteen, and Agnes twelve though evidently a more experienced dancer, for Lucy found her 'bathing feel' rather hard to overcome. She described the children's dance in her diary:-

> There were valses, quadrilles, galops, and two reels, the last of which we did not witness, being having some refreshments. But the first we saw, and very pretty it was. The Prince of Wales asked me if I could dance it, but alas I couldn't! His Highness danced with Agnes, and so did Alfred: happy girl . . . I danced mostly with Willy, galops, and every time we went close to the Queen and Prince; so near that I verily believe Willy would have twice punched Prince Albert if I hadn't drawn his arm back.

By this time the Gladstone and Lyttelton families numbered eighteen. There would have been nineteen children altogether, but for the death of Jessy. Eighteen lively children needed a great deal of attention and were a great expense to bring up and, as the families grew, the elder ones became invaluable in looking after the younger ones. With this regiment of children they could not all go to every party; they took turns.

For the ball to celebrate Princess Alice's thirteenth birthday Catherine took Agnes, then thirteen, and Lena (Helen), aged seven; and Willy and Stephy both had permission to come from Eton. Mary Lyttelton took Lucy, fourteen, and Winnie (Lavinia) who was six. The four girl cousins were dressed identically in white muslin frocks with ruches and pink trimmings, white kid gloves, white silk stockings and white satin shoes, and on their hair wore wreaths of tiny pink roses. Amongst the cousins there were similarities and yet there were differences: some people could not tell them apart. Evidently Queen Victoria knew who was who between the two families, despite the girls being dressed identically.

The plan was for Mary Lyttelton accompanied by Lucy and Winnie to come to 11, Carlton House Terrace, to join Catherine and her four, and then the two carriages would proceed to the palace. Catherine waited for her sister to arrive in vain, and knowing she had been very unwell and therefore might not come, did not delay and set off for the ball. At the palace Catherine found Mary with Lucy and Winnie had come separately, but noticed she was looking very pale and tired. The two mothers were entranced to see their daughters dressed in matching frocks with pink roses in their hair. Soon everyone lined up to pass before the Queen on her throne. Lost amongst the crowds of people and children, fourteen-year-old Lucy found herself with her aunt. She looked for her mother, could not find her amongst so many people taller than herself; she looked for Winnie, realised she would be hidden behind the mass of crinolines, and felt the best she could do was to tag behind her cousins. Catherine made a curtsey to the Queen followed by Agnes and Lena.

Then came Lucy followed by the two boys. The Queen smiled but as Lucy curtsied, she announced to Catherine: 'This is not one of yours!' To which Catherine replied: 'Lucy Lyttelton.' Lucy wrote afterwards in her diary:-

> . . . Her Majesty shook hands with me! And then turning to Auntie Pussy, 'and your sister, where is she?' So Auntie Pussy looked round, and said something about her soon coming and we had to go forward, for there were more people coming up. It was very vexatious, and Auntie Pussy was very vexed, for of course I should have come up with my own Mamma. However, I dare say the Queen was not angry, for when Mamma did come up with Winnie, she smiled at her and said, 'Is that another of your little ones?'

The eight children of the Queen and Prince Albert were all present at this ball, including Prince Leopold who was exactly three years old. The younger children wore highland dress. Lucy's evening ended happily, with the Queen's smile, which everybody found so very special. Lucy continued in her diary:-

> Little Prince Leopold retired after the first quadrille led by a grand lady. The ball was over at about half-past twelve, when the Queen came down from the dais and made a lovely curtsey to everyone. I managed to get with Winnie near the side of the door at which she went out, and got a dear bow and smile to ourselves. Then came the National Anthem. Then we managed to find our belongings and went home. Oh, how delightful it was!

At the beginning of January 1857 the Gladstone family; Willy at sixteen the eldest and Herbert, aged three, the youngest; arrived to stay with the Lytteltons at Hagley Hall, twelve miles from Birmingham. Upstairs, Mary was confined to her room, expecting her twelfth child shortly.

Lucy tells of the eleven Lyttelton children being joined by the whole tribe of Gladstones! Lucy, now aged fifteen, wrote in her diary: 'Oh, the whirlpool of excitement we are fizzing in. The PLAY is to come off on the 7th.' So that parts could be found for all the children, the eight youngest girls were all dressed as fairies with standing-out skirts and wings that glittered. Of course the actors exceeded the audience in this big family performance. Amongst those who watched they would hear the loud laughs of Uncle Billy Lyttelton, the Rector of Hagley, who came with his young wife. Also present would have been the children's grandmamma and her companion, Miss Brown. Lady Glynne was known as grandmamma against Lady Lyttelton, who was known as granny. Lady Glynne chose to live permanently at Hagley Hall. Her health had deteriorated and she was always tied to her companion, Miss Brown. Miss Brown had been governess to the twelve children of the Rev. and Hon. George Neville Grenville, brother of Lady Glynne. Granny Lyttelton recommended Miss Brown to the Queen as governess for her children; but the result was that Lady Lyttelton was herself chosen to become supervisor of the royal nurseries, while Miss Brown looked after Lady Glynne. Grandmamma Glynne liked peace and quiet, whereas Granny Lyttelton, like her son George, had a loud voice and liked to be heard. There seems to be much proof that Lady Lyttelton, who was born Lady Sarah Spencer, had a wonderful way with children, setting them to tasks within their scope and perceiving their individual temperaments.

Her favourite story of the Prince of Wales was when he was learning to write, which he found a boring occupation. He had just been bolted on his pony, which was supposed to be lazy. 'There,' said his teacher, 'you can hold your pen properly when you try.' 'And my pony can gallop when he tries,' replied the little prince.

The twelfth child of George and Mary Lyttelton was born at the beginning of February 1857, just a month after the two families had been so happily at Hagley. He was called Alfred and was particularly strong and grew up to excel at games. Mary survived the birth; everyone's hopes for her recovery rose, but she gradually weakened to die peacefully in August. As well as keeping her diary of events and comments, Lucy, who so resembled her mother in looks, kept another notebook of every detail of her mother's last illness. Hagley Hall, the gracious, solid house with the pillared portico, had made an ideal home for the large family. Her mother's gentle, acquiescent character shone forth despite much pain as she said goodbye to her children:-

> She spoke to me a good deal about her first coming here, very cheerfully and fondly, as if she loved dwelling upon it. 'I remember Papa showing me this room, and how lovely I thought the place'.

Following their mother's death, the children went to stay with their uncle, Stephen Glynne, at Hawarden in North Wales. When the eleven Lyttelton children, the baby left at home, sat together in church it was the Rector, their uncle Henry Glynne, who became so upset at the sight of them all he could hardly stutter through the service. When his own two little daughters had died he had buried them in a field on the outskirts of the graveyard. He could not abide the thought of children so young being in the graveyard; they were soon joined by an infant brother; also their mother. For his wife, Lavinia (Lyttelton) had died in childbirth six years ago leaving him two little girls, and now to see his late sister's children at the front of the church quite overwhelmed him. Worse was to come. Three weeks later the church was maliciously set on fire to what purpose was never known. The Rector and his brother, and William, courageously salvaged what they could, and saved pews, books and valuables by carrying them safety. The church had to be rebuilt and to this day certain pews are scarred with marks from burning timber falling from the roof.

Meanwhile Catherine was more and more busy with official occasions, and after a dinner party at Windsor Castle on November 14th, 1859, was proud enough of her husband to write a note for the family records. He had sat next to Princess Alice, who was then sixteen years old:-

> Dined at the Castle. William sat by Princess Alice — he was struck and much pleased with her, so unaffected and simple and very intelligent. She shewed a pretty rivalry about her own growth and Agnes's. 'How old is Agnes?' and 'then I am six months older and am growing still.' William in his answer acquainted H.R.H. that he had reason to know as he as Minister, and for the first time, had been present at the holy service of her baptism, to which she answered eagerly showing how she immediately connected the two holy services. 'Oh, then you ought to have been present at my confirmation . . . .
>
> The Queen spoke to me about dear Nora[1] and listened with deep interest about the end, and enquired about the other children. H.M. asked me whether Meriel and Lucy were now with me, and where our children were. Is Agnes to be presented next year?
>
> . . . . altogether it was an interesting evening seeing our dear Queen so happy with her children. The Prince Consort spoke about Oxford: 'I have been there lately to see the Prince of Wales. He sees your son, alluding to Willy.[2]

Agnes was presented in 1860, when she attempted to make a full curtsey to the Queen, and then regretted she had not had a better look at Her Majesty as she kissed 'her dear soft hand.' However she noted that 'Papa told me afterwards I did it very tidily.' In May she went to her first ball at Buckingham Palace when the Queen shook hands with Catherine, whilst the Prince Consort and Princess Alice shook hands with Agnes, and Meriel and Lucy Lyttelton.

> The dancing then began, and a beautiful sight it was to see all the gentlemen in their uniforms, and the ladies glittering with diamonds and finery of all descriptions. Then there was our Queen dancing in the midst of her people looking so bright and happy, with two of her children near her, the Prince of Wales and Princess Alice; and she really did dance, with all her own grace but with such elasticity and spirit, as if she really enjoyed it. Lucy and I danced once, which was more than we expected. The Queen was dressed in white crape, but her gown was so short that one saw her dear little feet very plainly. Princess Alice was in white also and looked very pretty and her manner so remarkably graceful and courteous I never saw anybody so wonderfully improved to what she was when I used to go to tea with her and the Princess Royal.[3]

When the girls went to grand balls they were seldom asked to dance, though they were more fortunate when they went to Oxford. Otherwise they watched their elders enjoy themselves which, though tedious, was only to be expected. At their first dance at the palace neither Meriel or Lucy had danced, but watched their Aunt Catherine 'partake of every single and kind of dance till she looked like death's door with fatigue.' Lucy, the very image of her mother with bright eyes, pretty features and dark hair, had an affinity with Catherine that increased with time. Whilst Lucy admired her she did not always agree with her. Like everybody else she noticed Catherine enjoyed meeting very important people, whom the family referred to as the 'great guns.' Since their mother had died she often took Meriel and Lucy to parties with Agnes, and the three girls all went with her to Oxford in June for eights' week.

Although Agnes had danced with the Prince of Wales before she had not danced with him since she had officially entered society, and this was to lead to some anxiety during the visit. After a pleasant afternoon on the river they dressed for the Freemasons' ball, with not much time for high tea there being only one maid to dress all three girls. This was held in the Town Hall and Willy took them to the top of the room where the Prince of Wales stood chatting to his other friends who had been to Königswinter, Wood and Stanley, who both danced with Agnes. However, when the Prince asked her to dance, she had to curtsey and admit: 'Oh, I do not valse,' to which the Prince replied: 'Oh you do not valse, shall it be the next Lancers?'

Agnes then found herself going off with the group to supper in a private room, and when she returned to the ball floor the Lancers was just over.

> The Prince then came up to me and said: 'I am afraid it is too late for this Lancers, shall it then be the next quadrille?' To my dismay, however, the Prince left before the next quadrille, and so I thought there was an end.

The next day there was a party at the Vice-Chancellors. Here the Prince approached Agnes: 'I must apologise, Miss Gladstone, for not dancing with you last night. I hope it will be tonight.' He then spoke to Willy; Agnes overheard him suggest they should go off together and have an ice but 'before this was possible the Prince was nailed by some bore.' Agnes had not planned to go to the ball that night which was in Christ Church but, since the Prince had asked her, prepared to go together with Meriel and Lucy, wondering all the time if the fates were going to be against her.

> Well at last we got to the ball, and in time the Prince asked me to dance the Lancers. I was engaged to Lord Adair, and when H.R.H. asked me if I was engaged, all I could do was to make a bow, and when he again said: 'But are you quite sure you are not engaged,' I could but repeat my little bow, so he handed me off, and when Lord Adair was near he said: 'I am afraid I have robbed you of your partner.' The Prince then remarked how long they were beginning and turned to Mrs. Bruce saying with his little funny way: 'Ah to the chaperons of course it seems long' — that was a little joke with her for not dancing. He did not talk much while dancing except about his stupidity over the Lancers, which are seldom danced at court. Once he said 'How I wish the others would begin first.'
>
> At the end he took me up to Mamma. She said: 'That was a very good dance, Sir.' He answered: 'Yes, but I should not have got through it without Miss Gladstone's help.' In one dance when I was in his set I took care in the Lancers to make him a different curtsey from the others, and in the last figure it was so pleasant to feel his hand comfortably taking hold of one, not just touching it.'

Agnes wrote in her diary being 'mad with enthusiasm for our own Prince,' but being more reserved than her own sisters, and certainly than the Lytteltons, she was more apt to comment, 'my feelings may be easier imagined then described.'

The visit to Oxford ended with the ceremony of conferring of degrees in the Sheldonian, and Agnes sat amongst what she termed the 'general company.' Catherine sat next to the Prince. Although the Gladstones were becoming well-known by name they were less well-known by sight. A woman sitting by Agnes happened to ask her, 'Who is the lady in the pink bonnet?' Agnes replied, 'Mrs. Gladstone,' to which the rejoinder was, 'A stylish-looking woman to be sure, and the Prince is talking to her.' To which remark Agnes controlled herself to remain silent.

4

The Prince Consort

What were William and Catherine Gladstone like? That was a question many people wanted to know, especially after William was made Chancellor of the Exchequer at the age of forty-three in 1853. At the time he was Member of Parliament for Oxford University, and when they attended a dinner there the ladies gave their opinions whilst the men were safely tucked away in the dining-room sipping their port. One Oxford lady noted:-

> The Chancellor of the Exchequer has an intelligent though not a handsome countenance — very pale, and black eyes with rather a sharp expression. Mrs. Gladstone is a ladylike looking pleasing woman.
>   . . . . He talks as he speaks fluently and solemnly. He looks a little Jewish but his countenance is lightened by a pleasant smile. He was criticised by the ladies after dinner, some declaring his expression extremely benevolent, and others sly. I thought it simply intelligent. Mrs. Gladstone vanished as soon as we left the dining-room, and did not appear till the men came up. I don't think her manners are particularly pleasing, but she is a fine, fashionable-looking woman.[1]

If the discussion was so frank, it was just as well Catherine had made herself scarce. Had she gone upstairs to repair a torn hem with a borrowed needle and thread, or had a button blown off her fashionable dress, necessitating that vital new invention, the safety pin? Or had she made her way to the kitchen to compliment the cooks? Catherine had a certain graciousness about her but she was not one for small chatter.

The important date for the Chancellor of the Exchequer was April 18th 1853, the day of the budget, when ruthless economies in public expenditure were announced. William and Catherine were asked before to dinner at Buckingham Palace when Catherine heard the Queen say to her husband: 'You must prepare a large budget!' Afterwards Prince Albert requested an opportunity to talk privately:-

> My dear Mr. Gladstone,
>   As our dinner was interrupted yesterday when I should have liked to have had a few moments conversation with you, you might perhaps spare half an hour tomorrow or on Sunday, two days on which you might be a little less pressed with business than the others. Let me only know the hour at which you could come.
>   Ever yours truly,
>   Albert.[2]
> B.P. 8/4 1853

The Prince was well aware the finances of the country were in a critical situation. He would have liked to listen to the budget speech, but had to be satisfied with reading it, and wrote at once with his congratulations:-

My dear Mr. Gladstone,

I cannot resist writing you a line in order to congratulate you on the success of your speech of yesterday. I have just completed a close and careful perusal of it and should certainly have cheered had I a seat in the House. I hear from all sides that the Budget has been well received. Trusting that your Christian humility will not allow you to be dangerously elated, I cannot help sending for your perusal the Report which Lord John Russell sent to the Queen, feeling sure that it will give you pleasure, such approbation being the best reward a public man can receive.

Ever yours truly,

Albert.[3]

Buckingham Palace,
April 19, 1853.

In this letter Prince Albert intimates he would have liked to have sat in the House of Lords, but when *Letters of the Prince Consort 1831—61*[4] were published they were edited with a heavy hand. Every sentence in this letter was changed: and the phrase 'and should certainly have cheered had I a seat in the House,' has been altered to 'your speech, which I admire extremely.'

Catherine felt a sense of relief that seemed dreamlike after hearing the very prolonged speech, and in a letter to Lady John Russell, the young wife of the Leader of the House, she admitted:-

. . . . After great anxiety one feels more as if in a happy dream than in real life, and you will not laugh at the relief to me of seeing him well after such an effort and after such labour as it has been for weeks . . . .

Then she added she had noticed the effect of her husband on Lord John's expression:-

I must tell you with what comfort and interest I watch Lord John's countenance during the speech.

As well as having a busy husband and large family she had become more and more concerned with the poor in London. The couple had made their home in a fine house at 13, Carlton Gardens, near St. James's Park and ten minutes from the Houses of Parliament. Ten minutes' walk in the other northerly direction was Soho where people lived crammed together in smelly, narrow streets; in rookeries, as they were called, for their small rooms were as higgledy-piggledy as rooks' nests. Those who huddled in the streets and outside the full workhouses had nowhere to go, and for them Catherine helped at a settlement in Greek Street. There the outcast were given a mat to lie on and a cup of coffee and half a loaf of bread morning and evening. William and Catherine may have been different in personality, but they both desperately wanted to help the poor and destitute.

In 1854 the family moved to a nearby house that was bigger and better, and preferable in every way, at 11, Carlton House Terrace. The reason for a bigger house was not so much the need for more entertaining but because two more boys had been born: Harry in 1852 and Herbert in 1854. The family then consisted of four boys and three girls.

On the occasions Catherine was asked to take her children to tea at Buckingham Palace she would silently but pleasurably observe that her's were taller than the Queen's. Each year the invitations to dine at the palace became more frequent, and William and Catherine were also invited to Windsor Castle for short visits. When they stayed on 29th and 30th November 1861, they little guessed that two weeks later there would be a death in the Royal family, for at that time it was totally unexpected by the victim, the Queen and, indeed, the whole nation.

It was a period when parliament was thrown into a state of international crisis over the American civil war. The great cotton industry in Lancashire was dependent on regular imports of American cotton, and the separation of the southern states was to bring the mills to a halt, causing such widespread poverty that it came to be known as the Lancashire cotton famine. The reality of the war was brought home on November 28th, when a mailboat called the *Trent* arrived in Southampton, having crossed the Atlantic. It brought news that it had been held up by an American warship that had fired shells at it and that four passengers who had come from the southern states had been seized and taken away. On Friday, November 29th, the full House of Commons debated these grave events precipitating the international crisis still further. That evening William and Catherine took the train to Windsor where they had been asked to stay by the Queen. Afterwards Catherine wrote a note recalling her conversation with the Queen and the Prince:-

> The Queen was very kind to me — amongst other things she asked me about my eldest son, where he was, whether we intended him to be in parliament. I told H.M. that I hoped so, but that it was rather difficult now. She asked me how many boys we had and what the younger boys were to be . . . . She asked me about the meeting today, whether I was there and who spoke well. I mentioned the Bishop of Oxford and General Peel, owning however that I admired my husband's speech — to which the Queen looked arch and smiling replied that 'of course Mr. Gladstone always speaks well.'[5]

On the second night Catherine found herself sitting next to the Prince Consort at dinner. This she had never been invited to do before, but she coped with the occasion with her usual dignity. In fact she was known for her calmness when in the presence of royalty, and was particularly adept at dropping a curtsey. To make a single curtsey was not difficult, but to curtsey to the Queen and all those who sat alongside the monarch at presentations, moving sideways and bobbing to each one with a smile and a flourish, was her particular skill that was often noticed and sometimes envied.

Catherine observed that the Prince Consort looked tired, but was otherwise as she expected. His conversation was mainly on the ill health of other people, but he seems not to have referred to his feeling of fatigue. Always unselfish and unsparing of his strength and time he had been suffering from increasing anxiety and overwork for several months. Intensely philosophical, he would weigh the pros and cons of any decision with a thoroughness typical of his German background. Though stately in appearance, he had never been robust. Then in the middle of November news of the Prince of Wales's lax sexual behaviour whilst in Ireland reached his father and mother. At least it was first relayed to his father, who wrote a long and embarrassing letter of reproach, and then had to tell the Queen. To make matters worse, he mentioned that he had to omit certain facts because they would be too distasteful for her. The Queen, who had only recently lost her mother, took the Prince of Wales's little affair in a way that can only be described as hysterical. On November 2nd the Prince Consort, now suffering from a severe lack of sleep as well as many aches and pains, went to Sandhurst to inspect buildings for the new staff college in pouring rain; insisted on carrying out his schedule, and as a result got wet and caught a cold.

Because Catherine considered it a special honour to be put next to the Prince Consort, she afterwards made a note on his conversation:-

The second night I was ordered to sit by the Prince Consort. It was the first time I had done so. H.R.H. was suffering from what was thought to be rheumatic or lumbago, but excepting the *tired* look about the eyes I should have perceived nothing. The rooms had been made warm on his account.

  The Prince was very pleasant, none of the constraint which he had when he talked to me standing. Amongst the things I remember which he said were remarks about Scotland. Its fine, bracing air, such a contrast to Ireland and Penrhyn Castle. He alluded very touchingly to the King of Portugal's death — 'They do not know how to treat these low fevers abroad as the doctors do in England,' or words to that effect. I assented telling H.R.H. about Lucy Lyttelton's low fever this year when with us, and told him that Dr. Ferguson showed great skill and supported the constitution with tonic and wine before it got too low. The Prince spoke of Mr. Cardwell's[6] fever, of his arrival from abroad ill, and that he believed he had been in great danger.[7]

The dinner had been on Saturday, November 30th, and when typhoid fever was diagnosed two days later Catherine must have felt alarmed with the thought of sitting next to him so recently, for she had suspected nothing. At first there was confidence amongst his doctors that he would recover, and when news finally broke that his illness was critical it came as the greatest shock both to his family and to everyone in the country. Even so the gravity of his condition was not explained to the Queen till very near the end.

On the night of December 14th, the Prince passed peacefully away, surrounded by his family and with several doctors present. As is well known, the death of the Prince Consort dominated the Queen's very existence for the rest of her reign. They were both forty-two years old. As for their family of nine, the three eldest were just grown up; Princess Victoria was married and Princess Alice was engaged; and Bertie, the Prince of Wales, who was twenty, was enjoying his independence. The other six children down to the youngest who was Princess

Beatrice, aged three, must have been badly shaken by the sudden loss of their father, but were perhaps more resilient than the elder three.

Both William and Catherine sent letters of sympathy to the Queen, and William also wrote to the Prince of Wales. The Prince wrote back a moving letter to 'My dear Gladstone.' Before and afterwards he always addressed him as Mr. Gladstone.

> Windsor Castle,
> December 20th 1861.
>
> My dear Gladstone,
>   It is very kind of you to write to me at this sad time, and I sincerely thank you for your kind sympathy.
>   The blow we have received has been as terrible as it has been sudden, and I have lost one of the best and kindest of Fathers, whose sole object throughout his life was for the welfare of his children and the good of his adopted country.
>   The Queen, thank God! has not suffered in health since the fearful blow which she received, but she is utterly shattered by it, and her future life will be utterly blighted now.
>   I have every reason to be thankful that I could be by my Father's bedside when he breathed his last, and was happy to think that he had not suffered pain during the fever; but now a fearful blank exists which never can be filled up.
>   I have not the heart to write more, and
>   I remain,
>   Ever yours very sincerely,
>   Albert Edward.[8]

The letter in the writer's own peculiar handwriting, at first so difficult to read it looked almost as if it was upside down, was dominated by a thick black edge surrounding the paper.

Three months later William had an audience of the Queen at Windsor Castle. At the time he was fifty-two and the Queen nine years younger. Afterwards the Queen commented in her diary:-

> Then saw Mr. Gladstone for a little while, who was very kind and feeling. We talked of the state of the country. He spoke with such unbounded admiration and appreciation of my beloved Albert, saying no one could ever replace him.[9]

As for William, who stayed overnight at Windsor Castle, he sat up late into the night writing a long memorandum describing the occasion, which he evidently felt was of great historic importance. Written on double sheets of paper bearing the Windsor Castle crest and bordered by an eighth inch black edge, his notes of small writing covered fourteen pages, and must have necessitated sitting at a desk till the early hours of the morning, writing with quill pen and by candle light.

> I was summoned here on Saturday by a message through Lord Granville and having arrived in the afternoon of today I was sent for to see the Queen between seven and half-past. It was in the small room where the Prince Consort used to sit that I was placed to await her, and the memory of many long and interesting conversations with all their associations coming back upon me

joined with a vague uncertainty about the Queen and about my own behaviour to one at once my Sovereign and a widowed fellow-creature to give me a feeling of uneasiness very different from any feeling with which I had ever before anticipated in her approach.

In a few minutes she entered with her usual simple dignity. After bowing I fell on my knees to kiss her hand. She took mine, held it for two or three moments and pressed it. She told me much by that slight action.[10]

The conversation opened on general terms and then the Queen asked his views on the Lancashire cotton famine. She then enquired after his wife and family. Expressing her great loss, and how 'the sun and the light had gone with it,' she told him 'it was the Prince who did everything so well and wisely.' She went on to comment that she lacked confidence in herself, and must have been a little taken aback when he responded from his own singular point of view, for he put the matter to Her Majesty, the likes of himself and herself did not suffer from a lack of confidence so often as from over-confidence.

I said it was not for me to dispute the low estimate she made of herself but referred to her large practice and experience and urged her to believe she would find herself fully equal, although doubtless at an immense inward sacrifice, to the care of Government. She said she would heartily do her best but she had no confidence in herself. I replied I could not but be sorry to hear her use that language, so many were the occasions when us poor creatures suffered from our confidence in ourselves, and so rare those when we really suffered from the lack of it . . . .'[11]

No doubt William discussed his audience at length with Catherine. In a letter to Willy, an undergraduate at Oxford, she wrote of the meeting with her own interpretation. Catherine loved and honoured the Queen, but she doted on her husband and always sided with him. She now wrote of the Queen's 'astonishment at his humility.' Referring to the Queen she wrote:-

As she said, she earnestly prayed it might be long before 'you are severed from each other.' He again kissed her hand and said, 'God bless you Madam, God bless you.' He left her astonished at his humility as he says it was impossible not to be deeply touched and moved by her simple and noble sorrow. To use his own words, 'I came away from her not only with heightened interest and admiration, but with a firm conviction that this trial, heavy as it is, and almost without parallel, will mark the purposes of love for which it has been sent forth, and that her future will be blest as her past has been and yet more abundantly.[12]

Catherine herself had an audience of the Queen a year later, in March 1863, when she and William stayed at Windsor. Like her husband, she wrote a note on Windsor Castle paper to remind her of the occasion.

The Queen came into the room where I was waiting for her — at the first sight so piteous. I went towards the door. She I think saw I was nervous and who could not be overcome, for she took my hand. After I had kissed her's, she drew me towards her and kissed me. There was something I can never forget in her manner, it was not only the exceeding kindness, nay tenderness, towards me — it went further. It expressed such depth and noble bearing of her sorrow in the whole manner.

Nearly her first words were these: 'You who are such an affectionate wife, I knew you would feel for me,' and she gazed earnestly with tears in those large loving eyes, and this seemed to me so Heavenly an expression, even a look beyond this world, and all the time such gentle kindness and submission.

She sat down making me come by her. Most of the conversation was about the Prince. She told me that she could only bear it all from feeling it was only for a time. She dwelt upon the loneliness now that the daily life had grown into such a habit so strong as to make it a very part of her life. That now she had no one to tell things to, that He, the Prince, had everything.

She said it was a great help to go on with her Prince's plans to try and finish and carry out his wishes. She answered with warmth and pleasure to my remark that the Prince had prepared and set much going, planned and made ready things which only had to be gone on with. 'Yes, this helps me on and there is another thing which helps me. It is extraordinary how I cannot help constantly expecting to find him — whether it is out walking, near some tree or some flower, or sitting in some favourite spot, or coming into the room, or hearing his footsteps.'

As the Queen spoke, she would at moments seem so intent upon the subject she would become quite animated with the idea, almost as if she was going to see him. Then at moments the countenance changed again in sadness.

Once she said, 'It is very difficult to understand how one so good and who did so much good, why he is taken.'

I said, 'Yes, but we see through a glass darkly.'

She answered, 'Yes, I know, but still it is difficult.'

I ventured to ask her whether there was not great comfort in the thought that he could die no more, could suffer pain no more. He was safe, and she brightened up, 'Oh yes, this is a great comfort.'

She asked me about my sister — whether she suffered much, and much about her. And when I spoke of it I told her how once my darling had said she had no idea that there could be such suffering, none whatever.

The Queen then said of her Prince: 'I have often thought that if he had tried to live, if there had been more nervous energy, he might possibly have got through it.' The Queen had before this alluded to his having no feel of death, and she reasoned upon it the more remarkable, 'that it was not like one who had not pleasure and interest in life. He was so full of fun, he had so many things in which he took an active part and quiet interest.'

The interview was brought to an end when Princess Beatrice came into the room for a second time. The tiny Princess had just had her fourth birthday, and was to become the Queen's closest companion. Catherine wrote:-

Princess Beatrice came in twice during the time and the Queen told her to come and speak to me, and to show her dear Papa's picture. The second time she came it seemed to remind the Queen that the time was up and she asked me that I must ask to send for Mr. Gladstone. I kissed her hand. I went away deeply impressed.

When William and Catherine dined at Windsor a few months later, on December 6th 1864, they were pleased to find the Queen in a more cheerful mood. Catherine was struck by the ease and charm of the snug family party, which included Princess Victoria, eldest daughter of the Queen, and her husband, the Crown Prince of Prussia, and made a note afterwards.

William and I were admitted to dine in private with the Queen; nobody else but the Crown Prince and Princess of Prussia, Princess Helena and Princess Louise. I kissed the Queen's hand upon first seeing her. Oh, how the sight of that countenance in its black garb upsets me! It was a round table. The Queen in mourning, and the cap is the same as last year, only she wore a large diamond cross. In the centre was a very lovely miniature of the Prince.

The Queen spoke cheerfully and was cheerful, only now and then a sad look passed over her countenance. Several times H.M. appealed to me, but more to my husband. One of the things which struck me was the ease and the charm of the snug family party together.

After dinner the Queen, who took an intense personal interest in people, asked Catherine about her brother, Henry Glynne, and his family.

After we had got up from the table to disperse, the Queen came to me, and in a very pretty way she asked after the poor Glynne children, and she spoke for some little time upon various subjects: the Duke of Newcastle, Lord Elgin, and the hopes of so many younger men. She asked me my husband's age, and compared it with Lord Elgin's . . . .

After a certain time, perhaps ten minutes, the Queen went away, and just before this the Crown Prince of Prussia told the Princess that I should like to see her works of art. She most kindly consented at once to take us to her room feeling rather shy, and then was very interesting then she threw herself into the spirit of what she brought us to look at. H.R.H. herself lifting down huge folders and placing the light to suit them. I have omitted to say that H.R.H. was lame that evening which added to my fears for having troubled her by the Prince's request for me. We all walked down the long corridors and found ourselves in these very pleasant suite of rooms. There was very little light, and she herself took a candle to light up her little statues. She said she had never been able to afford to have the casts made into marble: we have so many expenses with children and journeys.

Certainly the Gladstones shared with the Queen, as with the Princess of Prussia, the fundamental values of a full family life. The Queen had revealed her craving for compassion by saying to Catherine: 'You who are such an affectionate wife, I knew you would feel for me.' Yet was there not something more behind her remarks in what had become such a frank conversation. Had not their husbands much in common, particularly in their rather severe, puritanical outlook, and their wish to improve society by encouraging what are now regarded as the typical Victorian virtues of clean living, hard work and good standards of design and manufacture? Had not Albert and William (ten years older) worked closely together on numerous committees planning the site of the future buildings of the Albert Hall and Imperial College; and that the British Museum should be enlarged to such an extent that huge museums were planned in South Kensington for the decorative arts, for science, and geology, and natural history. If Albert had lived might the Queen have later supported Liberal reforms?

As it was she was taken over by Disraeli and then set more and more against Gladstone by the Conservative peers around her who opposed parliamentary reform, whereas Gladstone's ideals led him to refuse to treat the Queen warmly and to 'pet her' as Catherine recommended.

5

Electioneering

11, Downing Street,
Whitehall.
Aug. 13, 1864.

My dear Papa,

I sent a letter to Mama the day before yesterday, which I presumed she would show you, about coming into Parliament. I hear from her this morning that she does not like to do so, because it would surprise and probably vex you. I do not ask you to press her for it: but I will explain to you why I have a great wish not to stand for Parliament at the next election.

But first I must say I am very sorry if, as she implies, you have been under the impression that I did wish it. It is true I have never expressed a general aversion to entering Parliament (though such a feeling may sometimes have lurked in my mind) because, should God spare my life, it will probably be right that in the course of time the son should prepare himself for succeeding, however unworthily, the father, in public life. My only excuse for not having spoken plainly, as to the present, is that I have never realised the likelihood of being accepted at Blackburn, till a letter of Mr. Robinson's sent to me by Mama the day before yesterday, (and which caused my letter to her in answer) brought it vividly before me . . . .

I hope and trust this letter may not vex you. Were I relieved of the present prospect of Parliament, I feel I would work hard at law, or anything, and try and get some little reputation, which would serve as a basis for Parliament, when requisite.

Ever your affec. son,
W. H. Gladstone.[1]

Willy wrote this letter to his father frankly admitting that he had previously written to his mother on the subject. It was the norm for parents to exercise influence in the choice of their sons professions. Indeed, unfortunate Willy

suffered psychological expectations from his father who, although very loving, had taught him scripture and Latin from the age of four and found it difficult to bring himself to accept that his eldest son had not his own ability. He had none of either his father's or his mother's energy and drive. In fact, as his father later remarked, he was totally 'lacking in ambition or excitement,' but when as a schoolboy he had signed his letters to his parents, 'Your dutiful son,' he meant just that. His first priority was to be loyal and helpful to them.

Since leaving Oxford, where he had not achieved the first-class degree his father had expected of him, he had spent some time at home helping write and copy correspondence; and had also worked with James Lacaita in the library at Chatsworth, where a new catalogue was being set up. James Lacaita, 'the Italian

Englishman,' had been persecuted for his political beliefs and had introduced William to the fate of political prisoners in the Kingdom of Naples, and had taken refuge in England. Willy much enjoyed living at Chatsworth where the beautiful surroundings were to influence his taste for the rest of his life.

Now he had suddenly been chosen to stand for election as Member of Parliament for North Lancashire. No doubt he felt a lack of experience for such an offer, which he knew had only come about because of his father's reputation, for he was well aware that electioneering could be rough and rowdy. Apparently he declined the offer from North Lancashire, and then probably assumed the matter would be closed for the time being, but he was mistaken. His intentions were short-lived, for he presently found himself in the whirl of electioneering.

Lucy, who had recently married Lord Frederick Cavendish, referring to Catherine as 'Auntie P.' wrote in her diary:-

London, May 22 1865. There is great prospect of Willy standing as a Liberal for Chester, but it is a pity, for he is exceedingly unwilling, and has shown some signs of being at heart a Conservative! But time will show . . . .

London, May 22 1865. Auntie P. flew across to see us, her clothes tumbling about her; sat down on the floor, and poured out Willy's electionums, which are exciting to her as only she *can* be excited! . . . .

June 3 1865. Willy has made a good, spirited, modest speech at Chester, and is patted on the back by the Spectator. Uncle W. went there to back him . . . .

June 8 1865. After dinner Willy and Stephy turned up from Chester, where Willy has been hard at work canvassing. He seems thoroughly to have warmed up to the work; and has made one speech which has gained him much applause for its good sense, manliness, and caution. We trolled electionums beyond!

To 'troll' was a much used word for to chatter or sing out, and 'electionums' was, no doubt, a word invented for the occasion amidst family excitement.

In Chester there were four candidates competing for two seats. Those standing for election were the Earl Grosvenor[2] and Willy as Liberals, and Mr. Raikes and Mr. Fenton as Conservatives. The Earl Grosvenor was heir to the Marquis of Grosvenor, whose country residence was Eaton Hall on the outskirts of Chester, and sat in the House of Lords. The Earl Grosvenor, who was then forty, had been an M.P. since he was twenty-one, and it was generally assumed that he had a safe seat for 'whatever might be his politics, such was the respect entertained for that nobleman in the city and neighbourhood that he was sure to be elected.'

The fight was therefore between Willy, Mr. Raikes, and Mr. Fenton, for the second seat. Every day when Willy went into Chester to meet his constituents and make speeches he was met by abusive placards mocking his youth and he was either depicted as a little boy or even a baby. At least it was something to laugh about, but the meetings were often noisy. The *Chester Chronicle*, which backed the Liberals, gave out reports that the Conservatives had made 'daring attacks' on Willy, and that Mr. Raikes and Mr. Fenton had 'on the course of vituperation' hired 'vagabonds in frock smocks' to heckle him.

There was much excitement at the poll at the end of June 1865. The five polling stations opened at eight in the morning, and those with a vote climbed onto a platform where a clerk listed their names and choice. At noon when the local workshops closed for the dinner hour a surge of voters arrived, and at four the stations were closed and the votes were counted. By half past four some seven or eight thousand people were waiting at the hustings, the platform set up for the announcement on the Roodee, now used as Chester race course. The Earl Grosvenor had held his seat as expected, and Willy had won the second seat with a narrow majority. There was much cheering besides many abusive calls before speeches could be made, and the *Chester Chronicle* reported:-

> Earl Grosvenor spoke after much disruption. 'It has been said that the gentleman on my left (Mr. Gladstone) is the baby that has been nursed by me.' An egg here struck the Earl Grosvenor on the breast and bespattered its contents over his coat and vest. 'Thank you.' (Cries of 'shame' and loud cheers.) 'Gentlemen, you may meet me with arguments, but it is not worthy of you to meet me with rotten eggs.' Another egg was now thrown and narrowly missing the Earl, struck some of his friends in the back of the compartment. The scoundrel who threw it, being detected, slunk away.

The Gladstone family stayed in Chester till eleven that evening joining in the celebrations, amongst 'great disorder, as well as enthusiasm, eggs and earth thrown about.' They then drove the six miles back to Hawarden in their carriage to find an archway of green boughs and flags had been set up and a crowd was waiting. Even at this late hour there were speeches by William and Willy. A bigger celebration came a week later when a banquet was held in the village for the men to welcome their new M.P. Several toasts were drunk, including one to 'the Chancellor of the Exchequer' by Mr. John Bankes, a local squire, who 'avowed himself a Conservative.' Mr. Bankes was an old friend of the Gladstones but his congratulations were hardly appropriate, for actually William had just lost his seat having failed to be returned for Oxford University. He had entered parliament as a Conservative, and had been converted, with Sir Robert Peel his political mentor, to the Liberal programme of repealing the Corn Laws in 1846. His action was strongly disputed by his ageing father at Fasque, and his eldest brother, Thomas, who succeeded to the estate there. On one occasion Thomas, a staunch Conservative, is said to have travelled all the way from Aberdeen to Oxford specifically to vote against him. For many years the brothers were estranged, and it was not until the 1880's that they were truly reconciled and William was to return to Fasque where he had spent long and happy periods as a young man. The second of the four brothers, Robertson (their mother had been a Miss Robertson), had chosen to live in Liverpool where he was twice Lord Mayor, to succeed to his father's business interests there. As he was an active

Liberal in Lancashire, he made plans for William to obtain a new seat as a member for South Lancashire.

Only a week after Willy's success, William and Catherine found themselves in Manchester, where at a packed meeting at the Exchange William was adopted as Liberal candidate. Presuming that his candidature would be undisputed, a big political meeting had been planned for the evening of the same day at the Royal Amphitheatre, Liverpool. Tickets were much sought after amidst a day of great excitement. The Chester Chronicle reported:-

. . . . during the whole day the doors of the several committee rooms were besieged by thousands of persons anxious to obtain tickets of admission to the theatre. Long before eight o'clock there were vast crowds of people surrounding the building and every entrance was stormed. No one reached the interior without a fight, and the theatre was packed from floor to ceiling. The appearance of Mr. Robertson Gladstone and the Chairman of the Committee was the signal for a tremendous burst of cheering, but these demonstrations were completely thrown into the shade by the reception accorded to the Chancellor of the Exchequer himself; the whole assembly stood up and cheered Mr. Gladstone vehemently for many minutes, and the enthusiastic shouts of applause were allowed to subside only after repeated appeals . . . .

Robertson Gladstone stood out because he was 6 feet 7 inches tall, a head above William, who although now a parliamentary candidate was still the Chancellor of the Exchequer. After a long speech which no doubt enraptured the crowd, the meeting was brought to a close with a speech by Willy, who had joined his parents for the day, and who concluded:-

I think in almost every sense the Chancellor of the Exchequer was the man for Oxford, and Oxford was the place for him. (Cries of 'no, no' and 'South Lancashire.') I said Gentlemen, in almost every sense, but I make one exception, South Lancashire. (Great cheering.) He will now be totally and entirely free ('hear, hear') and I have not the least doubt on Thursday next he will be your member. (Cheers.)

Ten days later William and Catherine were again in Lancashire for the declaration of the poll. Catherine was becoming familiar to the fame of her husband, and they were met at the station by a brass band and a crowd who formed up into a procession. William was elected, but only just. Three members were elected for South Lancashire, and William found himself coming third, a very close victory. By now both he and Catherine were tired, and after acknowledging the cheers he excused himself, first of all, from speaking at length on account of what he termed 'physical inability.' However, spurred on by the sound of his own voice, he managed to make, as usual, a very long speech.

Several weeks of summer holiday in the country was enjoyed by the family, while Willy and Stephy went off to Switzerland to climb. Then followed a busy autumn in London, and then the whole family, except the two youngest boys, Harry and Herbert, who were still at school, went off to Naples for Christmas. William and Catherine and the three girls travelled back with their two servants in the middle of January, leaving Willy and Stephy to stay on for a short time. The way home was done largely by train and boat, but was broken when they travelled by carriage along the coast from Genoa to Nice, despite the winter weather. It turned out to be uncomfortable as well as cold and they were short of time. Mary, who was seventeen, wrote to Harry from San Remo, thankful for a day's stop on a Sunday:

> Here we are for Sunday, rather glad of a rest, as we have been travelling Tuesday, Wednesday, Thursday, Friday and Saturday, getting up every morning at six, and starting with no real breakfast — a cup of tea! . . . . Part of the time it was frightfully cold, and we were all nearly frozen, especially those who were outside, as it was snowing pretty hard! At Genoa which was one of the places we stopped at for the night, my bonnet entirely disappeared out of the hotel! Fancy, how extraordinary, as no one could have stolen it! . . . . Today we were all but upset, as when we pass any carriage our coachman always shows off tremendously and smacks his whip and makes the horses gallop at a run-away pace. But today we hadn't enough room, and our side went into a ditch, but luckily was prevented going over by the rock. If it had been on the other side we should have toppled into the sea!!!

The summer of 1866 saw the terrible cholera epidemic, worse than had ever been experienced before, but the people of London were much more concerned with reform demonstrations than loss of life from the deadly infection. Feeling ran high to the point of riots, and in July the railings were torn up in Hyde Park alongside Park Lane when the park was closed by the police to prevent people attending a reform meeting.

Before that, on June 26, a vast reform meeting had been held in Trafalgar Square. After the speeches had finished, a large crowd of people went up Pall Mall towards the Gladstone's house in Carlton House Terrace, whilst another large crowd went to the Carlton Club to let their hostile feelings be known. It was the day on which the government had resigned and feelings ran high. Mary described what happened next in her diary:-

> Huge Reform Meeting in Trafalgar Square about 9 p.m. Hearing an extraordinary noise, we found that ten thousand had come to cheer Papa. The whole of Carlton Terrace, all the way to Pall Mall, was crowded, all shouting, 'Gladstone for ever!' He was away, but being told it was the only way to disperse them quietly, we went on to the balcony and were received with mad cheering, after which the people went home.

However, *The Times* recorded the event in very different terms as to the way Mrs. Gladstone had responded to the shouting and behaviour of the crowd. William felt he must defend his wife and the crowd as well which *The Times* referred to as 'a mob.' After some deliberation he chose to send a letter to the *Daily News*:-

> Sir,
>   It having been stated in *The Times* newspaper of this day that 'the ladies of Mr. Gladstone's family accepted the honour of an ovation' on Wednesday evening from an assemblage which the

same journal describes as 'persons of the lowest-class.' I beg, without entering into any question as to the delicacy and propriety of this style of criticism upon those who ought certainly to be exempt from it, to say that on the evening in question, during my absence from home, officers of police came to my house and stated that a very large number of persons who were gathered in front of it along Carlton House Terrace and towards Pall Mall would disperse speedily as well as quietly if Mrs. Gladstone would appear on the balcony, and they requested that she would be good enough to do so. Accordingly, this desire of the police was conveyed to my wife, and she did what was asked, as she thought, for the public convenience, and in deference to the representatives of public authority.

I must add that Mrs. Gladstone and other witnesses were struck with the respectable appearance and good order of those who composed the large assemblage.

I am, etc.,

W. E. Gladstone.

In October 1865, Lord Palmerston, the Prime Minister, had died, and Earl Russell, formerly Lord John Russell, became Prime Minister briefly, then remained leader of the Liberal Party. In 1867 William Gladstone took over from him, and in 1868 he became Prime Minister.

During the winter of 1866-67 William and Catherine, with Agnes and Mary, now just grown-up, spent several months in Italy. They resided mainly in Rome, where they had an audience of the Pope, and then in Naples. As the party set off on their lengthy and tedious journey to Italy, we can imagine them reflecting on being proud of Willy being elected to represent Chester and the political campaign of South Lancashire. This was to bring so many changes to their lives for now they all were to get to know the industrial north of England and southern Scotland. From now onwards William was a much more radical politician representing working men rather than the graduates of the intensely Conservative and Anglican university.

6

Cholera

Few who knew Mrs. Gladstone at that time were aware of the extent of her foresight, and the power to calm self-detachment in times of danger and difficulty. When the wave of cholera broke over the East End of London the London Hospital was rapidly crowded with patients. The crush became so great that often one of the victims was just pulled off a bed on to the floor to make room for another to be brought in. Amid these scenes of terror and suffering and death moved Mrs. Gladstone, with no thought of herself or her own danger, and with a quiet assurance and calm that brought comfort to the sick and dying and courage to the over-worked staff, carrying off in her own arms the babies whose parents had died of the scourge.[1]

Asiatic cholera was first diagnosed in England in 1831. It had been spread by travellers coming from India through Russia and Eastern Europe, and probably was brought by emigrants on their way to America passing through English ports. The disease, which was spread by polluted drinking water, became rampant in the crowded streets of the East End of London in 1866.

Catherine had been influential in setting up hostels for the homeless in Soho since her marriage. She had by now also taken on much besides. Lucy Cavendish (Lyttelton) wrote in her diary after calling at her aunt's house:-

London. March 18th, 1864. Found Auntie P. out, and heard that she is more overwhelmed with hard work than ever, as she attends certain meetings at London House where the Bishop assembles ladies to associate them in different acts of charity: an admirable thing, but Auntie P. has undertaken to visit a hospital in St. George's in the East, besides three other things. And how is she to do that, and all her own innumerable kind deeds, and her season and societyums, and be deep in politics, and be everything to Uncle W. all at once? She looks terribly fagged already, so does he . . . .

Catherine was undoubtedly greatly concerned with the poverty and illness she saw in London. Their house at 11, Carlton House Terrace, which they still used when parliament was not sitting, was not far from Soho, and she felt that her position had given her special influence that she should use. She saw the need for her time to be spent in hospitals, orphanages, and hostels. This had priority over what Lucy called 'societyums,' although nobody enjoyed a ball where she would see important people more than Catherine. As a result of becoming involved with help for the poor which was never ending, she tended to neglect meal times. Lucy noted a typical scene when she called at 11, Downing Street, official residence of the Chancellor or the Exchequer, and found Willy, Agnes and herself having dinner without her aunt, who had probably invited her to come!

London. May 10th, 1865. . . . . I at No. 11, where the old well-known manners prevailed: no particular moment for going in to dinner; Auntie P. in bed and asleep instead of dining, and appearing late bedecked for a ball.

This was before the stress and worry of helping during the cholera epidemic. Catherine had taken up visiting the London Hospital in Whitechapel through her friendship with Catherine Tait, wife of the Bishop of London. It was the most famous surgical hospital in the country, treating thousands of accident and medical cases, but only the seriously ill could be admitted. In 1866 a new wing fronting the Whitechapel Road had been completed and plans were made for it to be opened by the Prince of Wales. It became necessary to cancel the official opening so that cholera patients could immediately be admitted. It was then said that the new wing had been opened by King Cholera, for the entire population was ruled by the killing disease. Nobody was sure how cholera spread, but it seemed to be infectious as whole families and entire streets were often stricken. It was far more sudden and dreaded than typhoid and diphtheria, which were common at the time, and often fatal. In fact it was spread by infected drinking water. Conditions in districts such as Bethnal Green, Whitechapel, Hackney, Poplar, Stepney, Mile End and Greenwich, where new industry had started, were dreadfully crowded. Often entire families lived in one small room. All water had to be carried from the local pump and often there was only one so-called 'necessary' for a whole street.

At the time the medical profession could not agree on the cause of the outbreak, and there was argument as to whether polluted air or polluted water was carrying the disease. In fact several pumps serving a big area were contaminated from leaking brick sewers. There was a well-known case of Dr. John Snow, certain of the cause, removing the handle of a pump in Soho himself, known as the Broad Street pump, determined to stop people drawing infected water. The symptoms came on rapidly and often led to a painful death within three or four days, or sometimes sooner. A common first sign was 'washerwoman's hands' caused by dehydration affecting the circulation. Vomiting and diarrhoea would be followed by cramps and weakened breathing, and the death rate was very high, few recovering from the dreaded disease.

The London Hospital was soon engulfed by the terrifying epidemic, and each morning Pickford's furniture removal vans were to be seen carrying away the dead. By then Catherine had been a visitor at 'the London' for some years, sometimes taking her daughters with her. The hospital chaplain, Canon Scott, wrote to her advising her to discontinue her visits, but she wrote back by return saying that she would like to help as much as possible and that she felt her presence might at least cheer the nurses, many of whom had been specially enrolled. The quality that made such an impression was her extraordinary cheerfulness and vivacity, and the fact that even in these terrible times nothing could depress her spirit. When she got home after a long day she amazed her family and her friends by her sparkling smile and humour which she could hardly ever keep under control. 'Her sense of fun was like a perpetual fountain bubbling up in unexpected places.'[2]

Catherine Gladstone, Catherine Tait and Catherine Marsh, all of whom helped at 'the London' during the epidemic, were known as 'the three Catherines.' They were all about fifty years old. Catherine Marsh, an imposing and strong-willed woman, was an evangelist and author. With practical good-sense she worked every day of the four months the cholera was at its worst. She was a friend of Florence Nightingale, and had had the initiative to open a savings bank for the builders of the Crystal Palace which was being re-erected at Sydenham.

Catherine Marsh already knew Catherine Tait because their fathers, both clergy, were friends. Catherine Tait was a daughter of Archdeacon Spooner, famous for getting first letters transposed; she was, in fact, one of five religious sisters. Her husband, then Bishop of London, had formerly been Dean of Carlisle Cathedral, and it was while they were living there that they had lost five of their seven children from scarlet fever within six weeks. First they had lost Chatty, then Susan, and later Frances, followed by Catty and May. By the time of the burial of one, the next had caught scarlet fever and was suffering from fits and delirium. The diminishing group of tiny children would sing before their parents:-

Here we suffer grief and pain,
Here we meet to part again,
In Heaven we part no more
Oh! that will be joyful,
Joyful, joyful, joyful.
When we meet to part no more.

After the sudden catastrophe of losing five daughters with scarlet fever, Crauford and Catherine Tait went to Moffat for a holiday with their surviving son and daughter, but were racked by the worry that people would not accept their family, thinking they still carried the infection. They were soon transferred to London and met the Gladstones, who were much the same age. Later two more daughters were born. Crauford Tait was made Bishop of London, and was presently to become Archbishop of Canterbury. The Taits and the Gladstones did what they could to demonstrate their belief that cholera was not passed from person to person.

Amongst the doctors Catherine met at the London Hospital was Dr. Andrew Clark, a young Scot, who realised the value of clinical research with a microscope to determine the cause of disease. Many people suspected wine, which was often given to patients, harboured infection; and Dr. Clark tested wine as well as water, which was, of course, the real cause. His conscientiousness appealed to Catherine, and he was to become her husband's personal physician. In due time he was appointed physician to the Queen, was President of the Royal College of Physicians and was made a baronet.

The speed at which the cholera epidemic spread and the sight of the dead being carried away in Pickford's vans nearly led to panic. At one time workers could not be found for the laundry fearing contamination, but just one stayed on and gradually they returned. Massive amounts of chlorine, the best disinfectant of the period, were used to clean the wards and passages.

Better-off people living in the west end of London were seldom affected since they took great pains to get water from outside London, which often had been carried great distances. If the disease was suspected, bleeding and opium were usually first prescribed, and the patient was fed on rhubarb and magnesia, unfortunately hastening the dehydration of the body. Then, if the patient survived, beef tea and negus, a comforting mixture of wine and boiling water, lemon juice, nutmeg and sugar was given. However, the poor families who contacted the disease found themselves destitute. Appeals in the newspapers requested gifts of nourishing food and arrowroot, beef tea and wine, and also bedding, cast-off clothing and baby clothes. A relief fund was set up at the Mansion House, and money poured in. The Queen sent £500.

Catherine, being on the scene almost daily, became concerned about the many children who had lost their parents and relations and had nowhere to go. *The Penny Illustrated Paper* reported:-

> . . . . a lady well known for her active benevolence is almost in constant attendance at the hospital and has taken upon herself to provide for all the young children whom cholera may deprive of parents.

It was soon decided that Catherine Gladstone would become responsible for the boys who had no homes, and Catherine Tait for the girls. With charitable money Catherine Tait opened St. Peter's orphanage in Fulham for the girls.

Two adjacent houses in Clapton, north of Hackney, that were for sale were considered suitable for a boys' home, and a letter requesting further funds appeared in *The Times*. With her heart so obsessed with the needs of the children, the writer overlooked an important point, and a second letter followed with the information the next day!

Sir,

A New Orphanage

I am anxious to tender my heartiest thanks to the kind friends who have already subscribed at this moment of great anxiety to the Temporary Home for the Children Recovering from Cholera: will you again give me your valuable help? I wish to extend the plan. Let us not be content with half a work, but make the home a permanent one, and establish it in good air.

The case of children left orphans and unprovided for are so overwhelming that permanent provision from the present fund would be impossible: therefore, I appeal to the public to support a free orphanage. The cost will be great, but not too great for our metropolis. Various schemes have been put forward in this trying moment, and public charity has been directed to more than one channel. Would it not be far better to concentrate these funds for one free orphanage, the foundation of which has been already laid by those kind friends who have so generously responded to my appeal?

     I remain, Sir, your obedient servant,
      Catherine Gladstone

11, Carlton House Terrace. Aug. 15.

Sir,

     I omitted to state in my letter which you were kind enough to publish yesterday in *The Times*, that any subscriptions to the Children's Home may be sent to Sir Samuel Scott and Co.'s Bank, Cavendish Square.

     I remain, Sir, your humble servant,
      Catherine Gladstone

11, Carlton House Terrace. Aug. 16.

Like many others who had helped, Catherine was presented with a bible as a token of thanks from the London Hospital. She was also given a cheque for £250 from the Mansion House appeal for her orphanage. The Princess of Wales set an example by at once contributing £50 to the new fund.

Later, Catherine would cajole persons of wealth to donate by persuading them to visit Clapton, and in July 1876 'a monster cavalcade' of twelve carriages belonging to those with money to spare left Downing Street for the free convalescent home. No doubt most of the party enjoyed the adventure, unusual to them, and the result was many generous cheques. A committee of men was set up to administer the home and, as was usual, a sub-committee of women held separate meetings. One of the houses in Clapton was used as a home for boys, and the other as a convalescent home for women and children. Few children under five whose families had been victims of the cholera survived, and the orphans taken in were between five and twelve years old.

After two years it was felt necessary to move from the Clapton houses because persons in the neighbourhood had been complaining of having a convalescent home for low-class types who had suffered from infectious diseases, which they thought they might catch. The orphans were then transferred to Broadlane at Hawarden, and the convalescents to a new house in Snaresbrook. The home at Snaresbrook was two miles north in a more rural setting, but fate followed the convalescents who were even less accepted after the move. After eighteen months the landlord refused to renew the lease because of complaints that the convalescents had brought disease to the neighbourhood. Knowing there was no danger of spreading infection the committee of the Snaresbrook Convalescent Home took the case to court.

In court the locals took offence, in particular, to a man convalescent from smallpox. Other witnesses recorded catching strange symptoms, much to everyone's entertainment. They all had a good laugh but the case was lost. The only solution seemed to be to move again. Fresh appeals for money went out and a bigger and better house a mile north, Woodford Hall, was then purchased, which was so successful that an article appeared in *The Lancet* praising its use.

Catherine's goal had been to have a convalescent home that was free and open to any needy person. Although there were other convalescent homes either a charge was made or, to get help from charitable funds, a reference from a person in authority was required. Catherine realised that the most needy were the destitute from the East End of London, who usually were unable to supply letters of reference and her wish was that the accommodation would be free, though a firm hand had to be taken to discharge marauders, usually referenced to as 'tramps.'

Woodford Hall was purchased in 1869. It was a large three-storey building flanked by two lower wings and was used as a convalescent home until 1900, when it was demolished. At first it was called 'Mrs. Gladstone's free convalescent home,' but she preferred that it should be called 'Woodford Hall.' She involved her family and friends in the running of it for many years; a nephew, Neville Lyttelton, was put in charge of finances. To her the people there were her extended family. She did not always appear when she was expected, but when she did turn up her affection and extraordinary vivacity and laughter cheered the patients and staff and she would often enjoy playing the piano for dancing and singing.

Catherine had already started an orphanage in Broadlane House in Hawarden in 1862, for children from Lancashire left homeless, owing to the poverty caused by the closing of the cotton mills due to the American civil war. In 1868 when the Clapton home was closed, ten more babies arrived, and room was quickly made for them by converting the stables at Broadlane House. Money was constantly needed, and when Catherine had people to stay at her brother's house in Hawarden she would invite them to look over the orphanage and ask them to sign the visitor's book, no doubt often anticipating a donation. Her infectious sense of fun carried all manner of persons along, though her vagueness could be exasperating. Once her brother, Stephen Glynne, waved an envelope before the family simply addressed to 'The Rev.' with the plea, 'Beastly Pussy thinks this will reach its destination!'

She also tried to help people find employment and place them in jobs whenever she could. A story went that she was on a horse drawn bus going to a convalescent home in Mitcham when she got into conversation with a man sitting beside her who wanted a job. By the time she had told him about a position and supplied him with a note of reference the bus had passed her stop. To her dismay she had to ask the man if he could lend her the money for her surplus fare. When he got home he told his wife, who was incredulous, that he had found a job through meeting Mrs. Gladstone on a bus, and that he had lent her money for her fare!

Very often such adventures had a happy ending. William would say of Catherine, 'my wife has a marvellous faculty of getting into scrapes, but an even more marvellous faculty of getting out of them.' When Catherine met a person whom she felt needed a meal or a bed desperately, she had no hesitation in inviting them to her home or her table. Sometimes the children were amazed as she brought in 'every Lazar or moth' to her home. She simply sat the person down beside her without consulting her husband or involving her other guests.

Another story records that she was given a cheque for £100 by some extremely wealthy person for a charitable cause, and at once returned it asking for £1,000, which was duly supplied!

7

Hunstanton and Eton

Catherine was concerned over sending Harry and Herbert, the two youngest of the family, away to boarding school. Mr. Church had moved from Geddington to Hunstanton in Norfolk, and taken his school to his new vicarage. This meant the boys would be further away from home in London, but it was probably the sentiment of a mother sending away the youngest of her family which was foremost in her mind. Willy and Stephy and the elder five Lyttelton boys had found life at Mr. Church's school at Geddington harsh, but they all went on to do well at Eton. Now the younger three Lyttelton boys were going to another preparatory school in Brighton. Catherine decided she would much prefer to find a tutor and keep her boys at home, and in the summer of 1861 she wrote her husband a memorandum setting out her reasons for having a tutor. She really wanted his approval for a plan she had already envisaged, and she thought that if she put the facts down on paper he might be won over.

For W.E.G.'s consideration

Harry was nine in April. I think Miss Sufret singularly ill-fitted to teach and manage little boys. Herbert will be seven and a half in July. By that time the two (Herbert being forwarder in performance to Harry) would really profit by a tutor. I want to show that if we found a really *competent man* who would come for £50 for six months and teach the two it would be cheap. If we found that it answered, the teaching might go on next year in London by the hours, and it is possible that by going on in this way until Herbert was nine the two little boys might start at school, say Eton, together.

Then if I prove it is worth trying a tutor for six months, the next question is whether the man I have in eye is a really desirable man. Assuming he is, we start advantageously so far as he has been enquired about for the Herbert boys he gave great satisfaction. He is a clergyman, very modest, fond of children, willing to come on trial — preferring to live at home whilst teaching in London — prepared to dine at luncheon time and not to be oppressive. His wife to live with her parents.

I feel very anxious not to send Harry to school till he is older. In point of expense I believe this tutor would be cheaper. Without one Harry must go to school at nine and a half. I am not now speaking of lessons alone but discipline. He will be above a woman's hand unless indeed our governess had the bump of boys which Miss Sufret is singularly without; and Herbert being forward and manly, is quite ready to profit considerably. At Penmaen I suggest having the tutor whilst Miss Sufret has her holiday or indeed, if preferred, he would start after the said sea residence.

    C.G.[1]

The note was to have absolutely no effect. Perhaps William felt that if a governess did not have 'the bump of boys' they would learn discipline better away from home. Willy and Stephy had learnt much from Mr. Church. Besides, he said, Hunstanton had the great advantage of being near Sandringham, and they could go and see the boys when they went on visits to stay with the Prince of Wales.

Harry and Herbert both went to Mr. Church's school before going to Eton. The number of boys attending was by now even smaller than there had been at Geddington, never more than seven, and Mr. Church seems to have become progressively more short-tempered. The boys spent long hours at their lessons, and still had prayers and Latin before breakfast. Corporal punishment was given by the strap, the whip and the stick, and the boys soon learnt the degree of threat each held. Usually a two inch by two foot leather strap was used and the boys placed an exercise book under their trousers, in which case it would have given them a fright rather than physical pain. No doubt they were mischievous; Herbert records how he collected earwigs and placed them in Mrs. Church's sister's work-basket in the private sitting room, but the constant beatings made them revengeful and bitter.

It is typical of children that none of the four brothers seems to have complained of the harsh treatment of Mr. Church to their parents, whom they wished so much to please. Catherine must have had her suspicions, and just before he left Harry once revealed his private thoughts to his mother in a letter:-

> Now for the first time I tell you that I do not like Mr. Church. I can't help telling you he gets into such passions and is cross directly we arrive . . . . I do not want you ever to read this loud to the public.

However, there were compensations. Hunstanton was in the country and near the sea, and they saw their parents when they stayed at Sandringham, surely an invitation never refused. There was great excitement on the day the Prince and Princess came over to Hunstanton. First, the gardener told Harry, who at twelve was head-boy, that he had seen the Royal couple go into the church. All the little boys, except Herbert aged ten who for some reason was not on the scene, watched their every move, as a picnic was unpacked from the carriage in the park. As good fortune would have it, Mr. Church was away in London. The boys were duly called to partake of the picnic, and by this time Herbert had reappeared. Harry wrote out the sequence of events in a letter to his mother:-

> . . . . Soon a gentleman came up and asked me if my name was Gladstone. I said, 'Yes.' He then asked me the names of the others. I told him and then he asked us to come and have some luncheon. I was very shy. However, I got up all my courage, and up we went.
>
> When we got close the Prince got up, shook hands with me and asked me to have some luncheon. I then took my hat off to him and then bowed and took off my hat to the Princess. Although I had never seen her before I knew her in a minute. We then sat down, had some luncheon, the Prince and Princess talking to me all the while. The Prince asked if I would have some claret to drink. I said, 'If you please, Sir,' as I thought there would be nothing but wine.

He asked also where Willy was, also whether I smoked much, at which everyone laughed. I thought the Princess looked very, very pretty and very well.

The Prince, who had such a charming way with him, enraptured the little boys by sending a note to request a whole day's holiday in honour of the Princess's visit. Harry continued:-

> The letter was to Mr. Church asking him to give us all a whole holiday in honour of the Princess's visit. I took it to Miss Brown. She opened it and sent me back to say that Mr. Church would be very happy to give us a holiday. She would not let me say a whole holiday because she said that she was sure Mr. Church would not give a whole holiday for the Queen. However, I forgot about it and said that Mr. Church would be very happy to give us a whole holiday.
>
> After the gentlemen, who were all very kind, had filled my pockets and handkerchief with oranges, apples, figs, and cake, I retired for good, first thanking the Prince, then making another bow and taking off my hat I went away.

Harry and Herbert, like Willy and Stephy, went on to Eton College. All four of the Gladstone sons and all eight Lyttelton boy cousins were educated there. Willy and Stephy went to Mr. Coleridge's house, but Harry and Herbert and all the Lyttelton's boarded at a house run by two women. It was to be the last Eton house run by dames. Miss Annie and Miss Jane Evans ran their house with firmness and ingenuity, for they selected certain boys to be brought forward to be put in charge of the other boys. To this day the house in Eton is known as Evans's.

Originally, it had been run by William Evans, the art master, until he met with an accident. He was painting a view and forgot there was a steep cliff behind him. He stepped back to study his work and fell; the result was he never recovered from his injuries. Though he lived on for many years, he stayed at the back of the house and was never seen. Thinking he would get better given time, his daughters took on the running of the boys' house. First, Miss Annie Evans ran the house for fifteen years, and when she retired exhausted Miss Jane Evans took charge for the next thirty-five years.

When Harry went there in 1864 there were fifty-four boys in the house for the demand was unceasing, whereas most other houses held around forty. If Miss Annie and Miss Jane were criticised for having too many boys, as they were from time to time, the ladies succeeded in using their powers of persuasion to get round the authorities. Willy requested of them that Harry should share with Arthur Lyttelton, but they found themselves sharing a cellar-like room, for every space in the building had to be utilised. There was only essential furniture and the place looked most austere. For many years there were Gladstones and Lytteltons in the house, usually four or five of them: once six together.

The majority of boys travelled to Eton by train. At the end of one half Harry felt the urge to take advantage of the famous express, the Irish Mail, down to Chester, as it was the fastest train. It went only overnight, but how he longed to travel on the fastest train. Enticed by the idea; he did not worry much about breaking school rules; he was tempted to leave after his last class on the last day, which lasted till six. He had to share his secret plan with his younger brother, Herbert, to get him to disturb the bed to make it look as if he had slept in it. The scheme worked. He managed to hop on the Irish Mail at Euston and, getting off at Chester, he slept on the table in the waiting room until it was light enough to walk the six miles to Hawarden. How pleased he must have felt at his achievement. Then a man on horseback was seen arriving bringing a telegram from his Eton dame! The message said: 'Where is Henry Gladstone stop Evans.' Harry wisely took charge offering to answer the telegram. His mother agreed that he had better do so, so he replied, 'Henry Gladstone is at home an explanation will follow Gladstone' but it never did. Miss Annie Evans said no more.

With the increase in the number and speed of trains accidents were very numerous and fatalities constantly reported in the papers. An accident occurred outside Slough station when the boys were returning to Eton in September 1870. Herbert was then sixteen. He got on the train at Chester, was joined by his cousins, Bob, Edward (later Head Master of Eton), and Alfred Lyttelton at Birmingham. Lulu Harcourt, another friend, got into the compartment at Oxford. Hubert Parry (who obtained a degree of music whilst at school), also boarding with Miss Jane Evans, got on at Reading. Arriving at Slough, three carriages were slipped, but as the boys were in the front, they were unable to get out on the platform because the carriage they were in went beyond the station. Suddenly there was the noise of an engine fast approaching, and the excess carriages were hit by an oncoming train. The front carriage rose up contorted, so that the boys were flung off their seats and Bob went through the window which happened to be open. The other boys landed in a heap, and found themselves sprawling upon each other and their top hats. Herbert wrote to Harry:-

> Suddenly we heard an engine coming, and it came bang against our carriage. I thought we were going straight over, as it was balanced between the two, but fortunately the couplings of the next carriage must have had the effect of bringing us down again with a crash.
>
> Bob, directly we were run into went straight out of the window, displaying more agility than I ever saw him show in my life. If the carriage had gone over, he must have been squashed as flat as a pancake. The carriage was a good deal smashed, the footboard and one of the springs broken, so we had to get out. I never laughed so much in my life as to see Bob go out of the window and all of us hustling at one end and our hats flying in all directions. Luckily for us the engine wasn't going very fast or something might have happened.

A parent of one of the boys, surely a mother, was furious to hear her son had nearly been killed, and wrote to *The Times* under the heading 'Criminal Carelessness':-

> Sir — On Thursday last, when the fifth form assembled at Eton, according to custom, a certain number of carriages were 'slipped' at Slough.

The man who 'slipped' them turned the wrong points, and ran the carriages through the station and right across a siding. At this moment an engine came along the line onto which the carriages had been turned, knocked them off the rails, tilted up and damaged the carriages, and threw one of the boys head first through the window. The other boys were all knocked together, but escaped with nothing worse than smashed hats and bruised legs!

The engine that came in contact with the carriage was coming out of the station, luckily at no great speed, otherwise the accident might have been as fatal as those lately recorded in you columns.

Your publishing this may cause a sufficient enquiry to be made respecting the accident, and cause more care to be taken in future.

Your most obedient servant,

A Parent of one of the Boys.[2]

How did it affect Harry and Herbert having a father who was famous? We find William calling on Harry when he was summoned by the Queen to become Prime Minister in 1868. On the way to Windsor Castle he had some time to spare as Her Majesty was out taking her carriage exercise. On leaving Windsor to get a train from Slough he found he was going to be late if he walked, so he boarded a horse-drawn bus. People sat and stood packed together and despite the discomfort nobody seemed to complain, with every available place filled.

Occasionally the boys were allowed to ask guests to breakfast. Both Annie and Jane Evans were staunch Tories. Of course the boys could not resist asking the Liberal Prime Minister to breakfast when he paid a visit to the school to lecture on Homer. He accepted the invitation. The boys asked intelligent questions with innocent expressions. Inevitably, the political discussion soon turned to argument, and the boys watched Miss Jane Evans voice her opinions, taking the upper hand at least through their eyes, as their innocent expressions became faces of glee.

Miss Annie Evans, the elder of the two sisters, first took charge of the house. The boys proved to be exhausting and she was walked off her legs. On one occasion Harry had been playing cards, in fact organising a card game, and of cards Miss Annie did not approve. Harry was hurt when she flared up at him, pushed him bodily away and threatening to report him to his parents. Afterwards, he told his mother, he had said in the heat of the moment that he did not care if a complaint was made to them for bad behaviour and then bitterly regretted speaking.

Miss Annie and Miss Jane knew that the boys would be unable to resist kicking footballs along the passages. To protect the walls, wooden boards were fitted so that the boys could kick their footballs if they felt they had to. All the Gladstones and Lytteltons were good at football, but the Lytteltons excelled at cricket. Not only did they all play in the Eton cricket XI, but all played for Cambridge University. At Hagley the cricket field was so close to the house that they only had to step out of doors to play, and the Hawarden Park cricket club was founded in 1866. At Eton boys had invented the game of fives between the buttresses of the huge chapel, bouncing a ball against the walls. Willy persuaded his uncle, Stephen Glynne, to build an Eton fives court against the high kitchen garden wall at Hawarden, so the boys could play fives in the holidays.

During the time Harry was at Eton his father did not often find time to visit him, but he wrote frequently. Harry treasured these letters, and by the time he left he had accumulated 150 of them. As well as bringing information of the family they gave personal advice. In the first letter his father reflected well on how a new boy would feel:-

> . . . . If any time you feel difficulty, remember that if all things were easy we should never gain strength by practice in them: difficulty is in truth the mother of improvement. If anything happens at any time to grieve and dishearten you, remember that such incidents of life do not come by change: but they are intended by our Father in heaven to form in us a temper of trust, resignation, fortitude: and if they begin early, it is that we may early grow stout to encounter the ruder shocks which come in after life . . . .
>   I am just going off to Balmoral and I must close. God ever bless and keep you dearest Harry.
>   Your affte. Father.[3]

The letter was signed, but Harry cut away the signature to give away.

Miss Annie and Miss Jane Evans had an unprecedented tour of office, for they ran the house between them for fifty years. When Annie died in 1871 and was laid to rest in the little cemetery on Eton Wick Road, all the boys at Evans attended the funeral at eight o'clock in the morning. Herbert, Bob, Edward, and Alfred were there. A portrait of Miss Jane Evans by John Singer Sargent stands in the school hall.

It seems that there never was an opportunity for their brother, Sam, to run the house. He, like his father and his grandfather before him, was the art master at Eton. To him is accorded an extraordinary life-saving manoeuvre. He was a very strong swimmer. On 4th of June during the fireworks by the river, he was told a woman had fallen out of a boat. He immediately swam off and pulled her towards the boat but with ferocity she kicked him away. Despite the rebuff he followed her and succeeded in bringing her to the surface a second time, only this time she was holding a baby in her arms![3]

8
Upper Classes

The cost of entertaining, and dressing for entertainment, rose to new heights in the eighteen-seventies. With the aristocracy still very much 'in the saddle', the Prince and Princess of Wales led the way in society, and of all grand balls the ones they held were the most splendid. In July 1874 their Royal Highnesses gave a fancy dress ball at Marlborough House such as their generation had never seen for grandeur, when no expense was spared. The Gladstones, finding expenses for dinner parties too high, cut down on them and gave breakfast parties every Thursday morning at ten, when a variety of guests would be invited.

When they held a dinner or reception at 10, Downing Street, introductions were not made, as it was not felt necessary. If you were fortunate enough to be in society it was considered that you should know other people and be known. To help those 'on the way up' to make their way, a visiting card at the time held a tiny photograph to enable recognition of the holder. This was called a 'carte de visite:' for French was supposed to be accessible only to those who had found their way into society. At dinner parties each lady was informed which gentleman would take her into the dining room, and if they had not yet met they would be introduced. They then trailed out of the drawing room through the hall and into the dining room, their hand resting on the arm of their appointed partner, ladies of higher rank going first. After the first two or three couples the remaining ladies were not unknown to get into line by making use of the elbow and the bustle, anxious not to be left to the end of the procession.

Dinners were lengthy and enormous, and consisted of soup, fish, and two

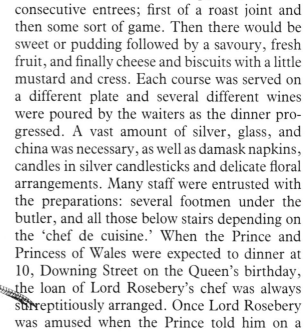

consecutive entrees; first of a roast joint and then some sort of game. Then there would be sweet or pudding followed by a savoury, fresh fruit, and finally cheese and biscuits with a little mustard and cress. Each course was served on a different plate and several different wines were poured by the waiters as the dinner progressed. A vast amount of silver, glass, and china was necessary, as well as damask napkins, candles in silver candlesticks and delicate floral arrangements. Many staff were entrusted with the preparations: several footmen under the butler, and all those below stairs depending on the 'chef de cuisine.' When the Prince and Princess of Wales were expected to dinner at 10, Downing Street on the Queen's birthday, the loan of Lord Rosebery's chef was always surreptitiously arranged. Once Lord Rosebery was amused when the Prince told him on a following evening that his table was much better than where he had dined the previous day. The Prince had the tact not to mention were that was, but Lord Rosebery knew. As he shared his chef, so he shared the joke.

Among the aristocracy Dukes held an extraordinary pre-eminence, and to have a Duke at your dinner or dance was counted the ultimate success. The last making of a new Duke was in 1874 when the Marquis of Westminster who, as Lord Grosvenor had represented Chester with Willy, was elevated to a Dukedom for his philanthropic work. He was a Liberal peer, so also were the Duke of Bedford, the Duke of Devonshire, the Duke of Sutherland, the Duke of Argyll, and many other aristocratic families, descendants of the Whigs. However, most of the big land owners were Conservative. Many of the people who went to make up society enjoyed the most atrocious tittle-tattle about Mr. Gladstone. To the rich he seemed a radical who was trying to alter their way of life. He was labelled a rascal, and those who worked with him were joyfully alluded to as Gladstone's convicts!

To many Conservatives anything the Liberals did was bound to be condemned. Lady Dorothy Walpole was a Conservative but had a gardener who was a Liberal. One day, wearing a hat and gloves and with her dress sweeping the gravel paths, when she went to inspect the greenhouses a shock was in store for her. In a letter to a friend she told of her dilemma:-

> I have plenty to do. I have got the nurseryman to rechristen a fuchsia he had the temerity to call 'Mr. Gladstone,' 'Lord Beaconsfield.' It had cost me something in orders, but the man promises not to transgress again.[1]

On the other hand Lady Russell, of that famous Whig and Liberal family, named the pony who drew her pony carriage Tory, and gleefully explained this was because he was lazy, stubborn and always took the wrong turning if given a chance.[2]

The eighteen-seventies saw elaborate and expensive dresses such as had never been seen before, and probably will never be seen again. For those of more modest means dresses would be made with one or two different skirts and two tops, called 'bodies;' one with long sleeves and a high neck and the other with shorter sleeves and the neck cut low suitable for the evening. Catherine and her daughters were never very interested in the intricacies of costume, and were apt to get their dresses made with a separate skirt and body so that they could be worn more often; sometimes two skirts and two bodies of the same material which were interchangeable. She was once away from home on a visit and changed her skirt but could not see that an evening body had been packed. Her ladies maid, Stume, had packed for her but had stayed at home. The only solution to Catherine was to wear the one she had for day wear. She folded her ample stole into a square and, with the point lying down her back and her arms well covered, left her room. Stume had carefully pinned the evening body to the matching skirt so that it could not get lost, so that Catherine was seen walking down a passage with the lost body flapping behind her 'like some sort of large bird.' She told this story of herself. Yet she had the inborn grace which enabled her to preside with dignity at grand receptions at 10, Downing Street, where the guests were served by footmen in red livery with knee breeches, silk stockings and buckled shoes. Sometimes royalty came:-

> Mrs. Gladstone is a very gracious hostess, and receives such illustrious guests with an ease and repose of manner peculiarly her own. Then supper or light refreshments are generally served . . . .

Ladies who wanted to read about the latest fashions and goings-on of society would look at the magazine that has continued until today, *The Queen*. It was then a weekly and carried a feature entitled 'The Upper Ten Thousand.' Lists of persons who went to the top social events were carefully drawn in order of precedence, Her Majesty the Queen and the Royal Family heading any list of events they attended.

On February 25th 1870 under the heading 'Ladies dresses worn at first Court of the Season,' we read of the family, as if they only just belonged, coming last on a very long list:-

> Mrs. Gladstone — Train trimmed with lace, white satin petticoat trimmed with flounces of Brussels lace; bodice of blue velvet. Headdress, diamond tiara and necklace.
>
> Miss Mary Gladstone — Train of pink silk, trimmed with white tulle, pink bows, and silver wheat, white net skirts with bouillonné and flounces, looped up with pink satin bows and silver wheat.
>
> Miss Helen Gladstone — the same.

One notes that Mary's and Helen's pink dresses were decorated with silver wheat. It was then in fashion to have flowers and fruits embroidered on dresses, also birds and animals.

About the same period it has been recorded that Dr. Pusey was walking down a street and saw 'a lady's dress in a shop window that would furnish a meal.' The elderly Professor of Hebrew at Oxford University had no notion of making a purchase, but his critical curiosity was to be amply rewarded when he discovered the price asked was £7,000. It was not only the price that alarmed him but the profuseness of the garment itself. No doubt it was embroidered with wheat, or bunches of grapes or other fruit, and perhaps ornamented with a bird such as a pheasant, or even a rabbit emerging from the folds of the train.

Where Dr. Pusey saw this dress is not in the records. A leader of the high church Oxford Movement, he worked in a dimly lit room in Christ Church, and always wore an old-fashioned tail-coat and a white neck-cloth. It seems unlikely that the dress caught his eye in an Oxford shop. More likely it was in London, where he was fond of paying visits to the Gladstones for theological discussions.

He was obsessed by the price of the dress and told Mr. Gladstone that he thought somebody ought to do something: ladies in society were spending too much on fine clothes. His comments made Mr. Gladstone feel out of his depth, so he suggested that Dr. Pusey should consult his wife.

The conversation had become a little delicate because what worried Dr. Pusey more than the decoration on the dress and more than the price was that the upper classes were wearing such very low dresses. Fashions were created in Paris and quickly copied in London. The crinoline of the 1860's had been replaced by skirts that were still vast and needful of a metal cage to keep them standing away from the wearer, but now they had a sheath in front like an apron which made the skirts even harder to walk with. Dresses were made using the most sumptuous materials embellished with trimmings and lavish embroidery. Miss Burdett Coutts, the richest woman in Great Britain (who enjoyed having Harry and Herbert to stay with her) was known to have a ball dress that cost £10,000; this having been made possible by having pearls and precious stones sewn onto it. *The Ladies Magazine* described the fashion of 1870:-

> Pointed, round and basque bodices are all represented in ball costumes, with the neck cut extremely low in front and back, and filled out to a decorous height with Medici frill of fluted lace, or several plaitings of the trimming arranged standing, and to lean outward from the wearer . . . . Other corsages are straight around the top, falling very low off the shoulders. In some cases there are no shoulder straps, the tiny sleeves alone passing over the arm. The thinnest tulle and gauze corsages have the material laid plain over a silk lining, and pointed corsages fasten behind and are laced by a silken string.

Dr. Pusey was all his life an indefatigable letter writer. He decided to write to Catherine on the evils of the indecency of dresses that were cut low. His writing was small and sloping, and the letters were rather thin, making certain words difficult to define. Aware of this he headed his letter: 'Upper classes and low dresses.' The letter began in a way which today many women would consider the ultimate insult, addressing Catherine as an appendage to the man he referred to as 'My dear friend.'

> My dear Mrs. Gladstone,
>   My dear friend your husband tells me that he had shown you the part of my letter which refers to the dress of society and that if I had anything to suggest, you would be glad to speak with me, whenever I should be in town . . . .[3]

Then he surmised to remind her that times had changed since she was young, and then make a recommendation that she, of all people, would consider ridiculous:-

> Why should not the good rich associate themselves for the protection of our young women, the mothers of the future aristocracy of England, that our young English girls might become again, what they were in the days of your youth. Thus if a certain number of ladies' mothers would wish to introduce their daughters were, in issuing their cards for an evening party to put (in

French, for the servants' sake) to the effect, 'It is requested that ladies should not come in very low dresses' or the like, I should think a counter tide of fashion might set in.

What the servants thought, or what they saw, also mattered to the Queen. In her memoirs the late Princess Alice, Countess of Athlone, wrote of a similar episode:-

Thora (Princess Helena Victoria) recalled how on one occasion, just before they went into dinner, Grandmamma (Queen Victoria) having concluded that her grand-daughter's dress was too low, pointed with her fan and said, 'A little rose in front, dear child, because of the footman.[4]

About this time Catherine took her elder daughters and elder Lyttelton nieces to hear Elice Hopkins, a small, slight woman who was a powerful speaker on women and children's degradation, and the author of several best-selling books. Afterwards Agnes and Meriel were no doubt lost for words, and for once Mary and Lucy were unable to write freely in their journals. Daughter of a Cambridge tutor who had brought mathematics to the fore, Elice Hopkins was a pioneer of the women's cause, and a follower of W. T. Stead (one of Mr. Gladstone's satellites) who had recently brought what was termed 'modern Babylon' to the notice of the public. Before this upper class women had no idea that such problems existed. She spoke to Oxford undergraduates on their attitude to sex which was unheard of for a woman at the time, but being a very good speaker and with a keen sense of humour she held their attention. She was a friend of Josephine Butler and Dr. Barnado. Later Elice Hopkins founded the White Cross League whose first aim was 'to treat all women with respect, and endeavour to protect them from wrongs and degradation'. It spread rapidly throughout Britain, then to India and America. Soon it had virtually spread around the world with groups in Australia, China and Japan.

9

Gratitude towards Mama

Since her marriage Catherine had become more and more engrossed with the poor in London. She did not hesitate in her endeavours and she was eminently practical. The poor needed schools, jobs, food, and shelter, and Catherine was looked upon as a person in the public eye who could get help by using her influence.

Whilst Catherine was taken up in helping the poor, William was concerned in helping prostitutes. It has been said that when at Oxford he drew lots with other friends as to which direction each one's sense of mission should take. The moral code amongst the upper classes in an age when the rich were very rich and the poor very poor, had a double standard and many people felt it was best to look the other way and mind their own business. The two pioneer centres for prostitutes who intended to reform their ways were at the House of Mercy, at Clewer, near Windsor, and in Walsall with Sister Dora Pattison, who set an example followed by other Anglican nuns[1]. The Gladstones came to know Florence Nightingale and Josephine Butler, both of whom held firm opinions as to solutions, and both of whom wrote letters of inordinate length to them.

In the middle of the last century there were no benefits such as unemployment payments and pensions for the sick and elderly. Women and girls found it difficult to earn any money at all. Those who had jobs in domestic service were fortunate; whilst positions as governesses and dressmakers were considered as providential. There were scant openings in factories and only a few pence could be earned as a crossing sweeper. Therefore women who did not have a man or children to support them had little choice but to go on the streets to avoid starvation. The problem of children exposed to prostitution was more horrifying but less obvious and, of course, children were often used as thieves.

At the same time as Harry and Herbert were at Mr. Church's school at Hunstanton, Catherine became involved with a parish in the east end of London where poverty was rife and was asked to find money to set up new accommodation for a school near the London docks. Although she realised that life at school for Harry and Herbert was austere, her worries for their discomfort were forgotten during a visit to the Ragged School of St. Georges-in-the-East, Limehouse. The Ragged School lay half a mile east of the Tower of London, and to the north of the recent building developments of Wapping. At the time the people living in this area were mainly dockers, with some costermongers — people who sold fish, fruit, and vegetables off barrows — and some needlewomen, who sewed in the tailoring workshops.

The Ragged School had outgrown its premises, and when she called there she was horrified to see ninety children crowded into one room. She was very practical in dealing with human frailties, and first of all she wrote the facts down in a memorandum, possibly so that she could record the extraordinary overcrowding to her husband:-

Christ Church Ragged School, St. Georges-in-the-East

In visiting this school founded six years ago for the most poor and neglected of the east of London, we find that there is a crying necessity for more space. The room occupied by 90 children is only 21 feet by 20 feet, and only high enough to stand up in. Sometimes 130 are crowded together subjecting the children and their mistress to disease from fearfully bad ventilation.

The scheme proposed is to purchase three colleges in the immediate neighbourhood of the present school, and to build a plain school capable of holding at least 200 children. This room will be available for Mission Services and Mothers' Meetings, which have already been found so valuable in promoting the improvement of the neighbourhood.

On a rough calculation £500 would cover the expenses. *Help* is *earnestly* requested, for their are no rich people living on the spot.

Those for whose special benefit the school will be used, with few exceptions are dock labourers, costermongers, and needlewomen. The crowding together is shocking: 712 separate families live in 296 four-room houses; the average size of a room is 12 feet by 10 feet.[2]

To fit ninety children into a room, 21 feet by 20 feet, they must have been crammed together on benches, with probably many sitting on the floor. The children would have been small and thin from undernourishment. There was no room for tables and the only way a teacher could have taught was through learning by rote and reading to the children.

Catherine at once set out to ask for donations, calling on people she hoped would help and writing letters. The memorandum she wrote, like so many of her papers, remained with the list of donors half completed. First, she tried for bigger donations and later she went after anything she could get but before long friends would offer to help her. Their offers would have been rapturously received, leaving her free to take up some further 'crying necessity.'

For many years she had been involved in running the Newport Market Refuge.[3] Before Smithfield Market was built the main slaughter-house and meat market for the west end of London was Newport Market, which was near the Seven Dials off the Charing Cross Road. Newport Market was used when animals were driven up the streets before the railways were built. It was closed in 1867, and bought to be converted as a hostel for the poor, the workhouses being already overcrowded. Catherine raised the £1,200 needed for the conversion. The halls and rooms were whitewashed and beds, either of coconut matting stretched on iron rods or simply floor mats, provided. A large cup of coffee and 1/2lb. of bread were supplied morning and evening. The places were taken up by persons who had been rejected by the workhouses, often suffering from exposure and exhaustion. It was free because the type it catered for were known as paupers, meaning persons who owned nothing. She ran the hostel and sought funds for it until she was over seventy. She wrote numerous letters to newspapers and chased after the rich for donations, often obtaining substantial cheques from Lord Rosebery and Miss Burdett Coutts.

On nearby premises, the Newport Industrial School was run, partly financed by local industry, as a residential school for homeless boys. It still fulfilled a need after the Elementary Education Act was passed in 1870 providing schools for all children, though not making attendance compulsory because many children had to work; when Catherine wrote another letter to *The Times* requesting funds, and commented on the committee 'enforcing parental responsibility.'

> . . . . The boys are all orphans or 'destitute;' no boy is taken in who has parents able to support him. Where there are indeed parents, but no proper home, the parent pays a small weekly sum (according to his means) for his child's maintenance, and this rule is rigidly enforced. If the parent fails to fulfil his obligation, the child is dismissed, the committee feeling strongly the necessity of enforcing parental responsibility.

Within a week enough money had been subscribed to enable the school to continue mainly in sums of between £1 and £15 annually; but Catherine was taking on more than her strength, her time and her family would allow. As well as having seven children herself, and protecting and defending her husband as much as she could, she was very taken up with her late sister's children, the twelve Lytteltons. Although she was so preoccupied with the feelings of others, she could not forget the child she had lost herself as she remembered Jessie, and how she had pulled up Neville Lyttelton over his manners. When she passed the large mantelpiece in the hall at 11, Carlton House Terrace it brought back memories of her husband balancing Stephy and Jessie, and calling for her to 'come quick and look.'

Already the Gladstones were considered slack and uninterested in keeping up with the fashionable London scene, and criticised for failing to attend society functions and for not giving enough dinner parties. The family seem to have kept private the feeling of being let down when Catherine rushed off to some hospital, workhouse, refuge, school, or orphanage, and had in haste forgotten them. Although she was quick to designate authority and responsibility, her success led to more and more of her time and energy being spent aiding the very poor. One evening Harry confided to Mary his great disappointment and anger. She, with tact and patience, advocated loyalty to their parents, and 'gratitude towards Mama.'

> As I am writing to you I want just to say besides my remark last night — the truth is we all

rather get into a bad habit of discussing Mama (as if we were her rightful judges) and it is only when other people notice it that one comes to see how wrong it is. You are not a bit worse than I am, but it is the only way we can help each other, if we now and then we pull each other up. Though I know it wants a great deal of patience and good temper not to be angry when one is pulled up. So don't mind my telling you this. I don't think you will mind, though, and I know you will try and remember how gratitude towards Mama ought to outweigh all other feelings, and how we should strive (if we think her in the wrong sometimes) to hide it from the world.

Then before long there would be something to laugh at, for some stories told of Catherine must be true, because nobody could have made them up. Once when she went to a grand party she looked at the hot-house fruit piled up in front of her and, self-forgetful as ever, took a piece to give one of her orphans, and put it in her pocket: her pocket was in the bustle of her dress. The inevitable happened when she sat down!

10
Louise

A vast statue of Queen Victoria stands in front of Buckingham Palace encircled by busy traffic. It is unfortunate that a very much more attractive statue in front of Kensington Palace remains comparatively unknown. It is the work of the Queen's fourth daughter, Princess Louise. The Queen, still young and slim, is sitting crowned on her throne, illustrious and composed. The tilt of the head, the cheeks and the mouth reveal a inner glow, an affectionate link between the sitter and the sculptress; and inner smile. When the statue was first viewed by the public people said it could not possibly have been done by Princess Louise; she was a Princess! The Queen, however, realised that she had a gifted daughter who had insisted on working without assistance, for she had a very strong personality. Queen Victoria was very fond of Louise but knew her fourth daughter meant to have her own way. In looks there was a striking resemblance between Louise and her father, and like him she developed a love of art and craftsmanship. She had been named after his mother whom she resembled. It must have taken courage and not a little persuasion for Louise to be allowed to take lessons in sculpture.

When Mr. Gladstone was taken ill in 1868, the Queen asked Louise to write on her behalf a letter to Mrs. Gladstone[1], for it seems that a special affinity had developed between this daughter and Catherine. The Gladstones had several small statues in their London House, including Italian bronze and carved wood figures, and a lovely marble head and shoulders of Catherine by Laurence Macdonald executed in Rome just before their marriage. It was decided that the Princess should be invited to a family breakfast at 11, Carlton House Terrace. She was the first of the royal family to receive such an informal invitation. It was not easy for the children of the Queen to form friendships, and it was especially hard for the girls, who were educated by governesses and tutors at home, and were apt to find themselves chatting to people old enough to be their parents at drawing rooms, as the receptions in the Palace were known. A date was arranged at the beginning of July 1870.

There was an air of excitement as the carriage was heard and the Princess entered 11, Carlton House Terrace. The rooms were crammed with pictures, furniture and ornaments; the guests found it quite difficult to move about. In particular, the edges of the rooms displayed cluttered shelves of china, for William had gradually amassed a big collection, which sadly

he was obliged to sell at the outset of his third premiership. There was English, Italian, German, and French china, for when he saw a piece that would enhance his collection he was usually tempted to buy it, and he was widely known for his interest in porcelain and acknowledged as 'a connoisseur of authority.[2] Yet what probably struck Princess Louise who, after all had come to see the statues, was the vast quantity of pictures.

The rooms although very large were not vast, and the most valuable picture was so immense it would have ruled supreme in any private house. It measured 9 feet by 6 feet, and was of the Virgin and St. John the Baptist, by Bonifazio.[3] There was Christ and the Apostles, by Mantegna;[3] St. Francis of Paola, by Murillo;[3] the Capitol of Rome, by Canaletto;[3] and many other very valuable Italian paintings.[4] In addition the house held many large pictures by British artists recently done, several of which had been purchased directly from exhibitions at the Royal Academy in Piccadilly. As with the porcelain, most of the collection had later to be sold in order to support the expenses of high office, and was sent for auction at Christies.

Perhaps the Princess found it difficult to concentrate on the pictures, statues and china, for at the breakfast party she had got to know a good-looking young man who was working as a private secretary to her host, who although at that time Prime Minister had kept on the family house. It was a few days before she wrote a letter of thanks:-

Osborne.
15 July 1870.

Dear Mrs. Gladstone,

    I have been wanting to write to you so much, but not until now have I had a moment to myself to do so. I have been anxious to express to Mr. Gladstone and yourself, what a great pleasure it was to me coming to your breakfast on Monday, and how very much I enjoyed it and how much I felt the kindness which was shown to me. There were so many people there I had been so anxious to become acquainted with, so you can judge how pleased I was when I saw them. Also your husband's treasures were most interesting to me.

        Ever with many thanks,
           Yours very sincerely,
           Louise.[5]

In her letter the Princess said she had met people she 'had been so anxious to become acquainted with,' but she did not reveal all her thoughts; for she had fallen in love with Lord Lorne. Lord Lorne was the eldest son of the large family of the Duke of Argyle, short, red-headed, and a fiery speaker in the House of Lords for the Liberal cause. Both Lorne's father and his mother, who was daughter of the Duke and Duchess of Sutherland, knew the Gladstones well. The Queen had previously told Louise that Lorne would make a suitable match, but she had been unsure.

It was a whirlwind romance for by the time the Queen asked Louise who she would like to invite to Balmoral in the autumn, her intentions must have been open to suspicion. Here at least there was a little freedom for the friendship to develop; even so the two were probably never left alone to enjoy each other's company in private. The engagement took place on a day the Queen described as 'perfectly cloudless.' She recorded in her journal for October 3rd:-

This was an eventful day! Our dear Louise was engaged to Lord Lorne.

The event took place during a walk from the Glassalt Shiel to the Dem Loch. She had gone there with Janie Ely, the Lord Chancellor (Lord Hatherley), and Lorne. I had driven with Beatrice and the Hon. Mrs. Ponsonby to Pannanich Wells, two miles from Ballater, on the south side of the Dee where I had been many years ago.

. . . . The same perfectly cloudless sky as on the two proceeding days. We got home by seven. Louise, who returned some time after we did, told me that Lorne had spoken of his devotion to her, and proposed to her, and that she had accepted him, knowing that I would approve. Though I was not unprepared for this result, I felt painfully the thought of losing her. But I naturally gave my consent, and could only pray that she might be happy.[6]

The sudden announcement of Princess Louise's engagement came as a big surprise to the British public. Those who knew her, or thought they did, said it was amazing, astonishing and wondered how she would manage; for the fourth of five sisters, her elder three sisters having married husbands of royal birth, all of whom were German, was to marry a mere Scottish nobleman. Anybody overhearing the tittle-tattle that took place in London drawing-rooms might have thought a scandal had taken place. However, once the engagement was announced there was never any doubt that the marriage would go ahead. In parliament the Marquis of Westminster 'expressed the delight of the House that, after three of the Queen's daughters had gone to live in Germany, one should go to Scotland.'[7]

The Gladstones were much excited by the news of the engagement, for they felt partly responsible, and we can imagine Catherine would have treated the news with cries of 'what a break,' to be echoed by her daughters with 'a break plus!' But it was not enough to simply speak one's congratulations. Letters of good wishes had to be thoughtfully written and answered:-

Balmoral Castle,
18 Oct '70.

Dear Mrs. Gladstone,

Many thanks for your kind good wishes on your hearing of my engagement.

I was *much touched* by Mr. Gladstone's letter to the Queen. I feel these words coming from *him* mean a great deal more, far more than we deserve, Lorne and I think.

I think we shall be very happy, and we shall have pride in overcoming the difficulties which everybody places before us, every position has its difficulties, why should we not be without them?

That I am not leaving my own dear Country is a great joy to me. We hope to lead a life of usefulness.

With renewed thanks for your many good wishes,

Yours,

Louise.[8]

After reading this Catherine retorted: 'how can people assure her she will have difficulties?'

On the other hand Lord Lorne, probably little aware of the difficulties 'everybody' was putting before Louise, wrote in a charming letter that he was overcome with happiness and people's kindness:-

Inveraray.
October 22, 1870.

Dear Mrs. Gladstone,

I feel so miserably undeserving of my happiness and people's kindness! It is very good of you to write to me after the dear letter you sent my mother . . . .

I think it is not a little owing to your kindness in asking me to your pleasant breakfast party in London, that things have fallen out as they have.

You know Princess Louise is one of somebody's greatest admirers — and I think you will agree with me that is only one of the things in which she shows wisdom!

Ever dear Mrs. Gladstone,
Yours affectionately,
Lorne.[9]

The match between the Queen's daughter and the Scottish aristocrat was a true love-story, but it is unlikely they knew each other well. Of course the Princess's upbringing had been narrow and protective, but so had Lord Lorne's. Instead of attending school and university his parents sent him off at an early age in a travelling carriage, with a tutor, a courier and a personal servant, to be educated abroad, principally in Italy. Although Lorne would inherit his father's property, gossip insisted that he was not rich enough to marry the Queen's daughter. Then, as if this was not a sufficiently grave problem, the gossipers proceeded gleefully to enquire how they would cope for titles, his and hers and, of more serious consequence, how they would manage for rank.

Throughout the country there was active discussion between members of parliament and their constituents as to how much the royal grant should be, seemingly all other matters taking second place. Then, amongst women there was much guessing over the fashions Princess Louise would choose. Sewing machines had recently been invented employing thousands of women, and there was feverish speculation over the bride's trousseau. Would she wear the crinoline or the bustle? Would the skirt be held out by a steel frame? In the parlance of dressmakers, would she wear steels or the straight up-and-down?

The wedding was to be in March at Windsor, and William, Catherine, Agnes, and Mary were all invited to stay at the Castle for a few days in February. Mary, a close friend of Princess Louise's, and her parents dined with the Queen, whilst Agnes found herself in the lesser dining room of the Queen's household. On the evening that Catherine sat next to the Queen, Mary noted:-

H.M. talks a good deal to Princess Louise aside, and they must have a keen sense of the ridiculous from the way they laughed . . . . She thinks Lord Westminster had an absurd mania for pulling down and altering. After dinner we stood around rather like fools, and after a few minutes' conversation with Lady Churchill, H.M. came up to me and began talking about Herbert's illness; also wanting to know how far Ida suffered now from her accident. Then asked about Helen, where she was . . . .

Herbert had had peritonitis at Eton, and formerly the Queen had recommended that on no account should he ever row again. Ida, a cousin[10], had been tragically injured when she had hit her head on an overhanging branch when her horse had bolted. Although the accident had happened at her home in Scotland, she was being treated at Roehampton Hospital.

The wedding was planned to be a splendid occasion in St. George's Chapel, Windsor, with many more guests than had attended the marriages of the other Princesses. The Princess Royal had been married in the Chapel Royal, St. James's; Princess Alice at Osborne, and Princess Helena in the private chapel at Windsor. From *The Times* we learn that the 21st March had spring-like sunshine and that the crowd at Windsor was well-behaved for 'there was a conspicuous and agreeable absence of the rough element, which forms such a very obnoxious feature in a London crowd. A comparatively small force of constables was sufficient to keep the line of the route clear for the wedding guests.' Catherine was outstanding in 'deep blue silk, richly trimmed with velvet,' wearing her diamond necklace and her hair in blondé — silk lace with hexagonal meshes — with velvet ribbons and blue feathers.[11] The men wore court uniform. The Gladstones sat, prominently placed, in the Knights' stalls.

When the Prince of Wales had married in St. George's chapel eight years previously the Queen, recently widowed, had secluded herself in a balcony and had not attended the reception afterwards. Evidently, the Queen felt very differently for this wedding, for when the organ announced the procession of the bride she walked up the aisle with the Queen, who was giving her daughter in marriage. The interior of St. George's gives a tremendous feeling of space and height and, as the congregation turned to watch, the couple would have been conspicuous for their small size: the Queen less than five feet and Princess Louise a little taller, but nevertheless small and slim. They were followed by eight bridesmaids. The Queen wore a black satin dress with pleated flounces and black lace, and on her head a diadem of diamonds holding in place her long white tulle veil. The bride's dress was of heavy white satin, very ornate, full, and cumbersome with a large train. Although the train and shorter overskirt was of rich Honiton lace, the main skirt and deep collar were embellished with life-like silk flowers, and her head held a wreath of similar silk flowers of orange blossom, myrtle and white heather. Her dark hair, loosely curled, fell below her shoulders and she wore a single strand necklace of immense pearls; the Queen's usual custom being of giving her daughters one or two pearls each year; and from the pearls a pendant of a flying angel. Had not the romantic bride called her husband an angel? One of the most touching gifts she had received had come from the three members of the family who were younger than her: Prince Arthur, Prince Leopold and Princess Beatrice; who together had given her two diamond clasps in the form of daisies to fasten her veil of heavy Honiton lace.

Afterwards there was a wedding breakfast at 2.15 in the oak room for sixty guests, and a standing luncheon in the Waterloo Chamber for 'the general company' of some three or four hundred, and then the couple left for Claremont in Esher. At 4.30 a carriage drew up and the happy couple, for this had been the happiest of weddings, sat in the open carriage. Louise must have looked a picture dressed in white Irish corded linen trimmed with swansdown and a chip straw bonnet trimmed with lilies of the valley and orange blossom. The carriage had an escort of Lifeguards on their black chargers, and drew away through Windsor Park by the Long Walk, which for a mile was continuously thronged with well-wishers.

For the next few years Lord Lorne was an active Member of Parliament and then, after all, the couple went to live abroad. For in 1878 Lord Lorne was made Governor-General of Canada, and the Province of Alberta was named after his wife, Alberta being her third name. Sadly the couple never had children, and Princess Louise suffered a terrible accident in Canada falling from a moving sleigh, from which she never recovered. After three years they returned from their tour of duty in 1881, by which time Prince Leopold had made up his mind to become the next Governor-General of Canada.

11
Leopold

Prince Leopold spent much time resting on a sofa at Buckingham Palace whilst the other royal children were up and about, for he was a victim of haemophilia, so that when he knocked himself or fell over his bruises took a long time to heal. He was the fourth son and eighth child of the Queen and Prince Albert. For his birth the Queen was relieved with chloroform for the first time, thereafter making the method acceptable for countless thankful mothers.

The Queen was unaware that she carried the faulty gene of the dreaded condition, and the shock to her and Prince Albert on hearing of the diagnosis of haemophilia can only be imagined. Leopold was always delicate but they hoped he might miraculously grow out of his condition. Meanwhile, they followed the doctors' advice that he must rest. Because of his disability he was not given a commission in the army or Navy like his brothers.

When eminent persons called to have an audience of the Queen they often found time to have a chat with the young Prince resting on a sofa. They quickly discovered that he had a happy disposition, was not shy, talked intelligently and had an interest in beautiful objects: china, furniture and pictures. When Mr. Gladstone found out that Prince Leopold was interested in china the discussion led to Wedgwood. Ever since his marriage William had collected china, and he was known as an authority on the life of Josiah Wedgwood. He had known Leopold from childhood, who seems to have found him pompous but kindly, and they appear to have established a trust in each other.

Following the conversation William decided to send a pamphlet of a talk he

had given on Wedgwood china, together with a letter praising Josiah Wedgwood as being 'the man most remarkable for combining art and commerce.' Prince Leopold replied: 'I have a great veneration for Wedgwood himself; and I value your book all the more as I have never seen any written account of him and his life.[1]

William realised that Prince Leopold and Josiah Wedgwood by a strange coincidence suffered from a similar affliction. Prince Leopold's handicap was a recurring swollen and painful right knee, whereas Josiah Wedgwood had a painful infection on his right leg and had to work at the potter's wheel with his leg elevated. At the age of sixteen he had caught smallpox and as a result never grew up to reach his normal strength. Later the infection on his right leg spread necessitating amputation and, lacking the essential balance, he was no longer able to throw pots. Up to this time he had been a thrower; that is to say his job was to throw the lump of clay onto the centre of the wheel and fashion the required article between fingers and thumb. The wheel, incidentally, was turned by a boy or girl, providing employment for children who were thankful to earn a few pence to help feed their families.

The pamphlet on Josiah Wedgwood was the speech — it must have been a very long speech — that William had given at the opening of the Wedgwood Memorial Institute in 1863. He told how Josiah Wedgwood, after the trauma of losing his leg, studied both pottery design and the composition of clay, resulting in the factory producing china that was both beautiful and durable. This led to the firm becoming so prosperous that they had eventually been able to build the Wedgwood Memorial Institute. It was to be a museum, a school of art and a free library 'not only for the public of the district, but the nation at large.'

We can imagine a crowd of workmen listening at the opening ceremony, the speaker elevated for all to see, telling them how brilliant Josiah Wedgwood had been, and how their prosperity was due to him: finally, the speaker describing some of his own collection with infectious enthusiasm. His favourite set of Wedgwood china consisted of a milk jug and lid, sugar dish with cover, and cup and saucer on a china tray, that came from a service made for Queen Charlotte. There was rapture of delight as he described this set, called a 'déjeuner,' specially made for Queen Charlotte to enjoy a little warm milk.

> I have a déjeuner, nearly slate coloured, of the ware which, I believe, is called jasper ware. This seems to me a perfect model of workmanship and taste. The tray is a short oval, extremely light with a surface as soft as an infant's flesh to the touch, and having for ornament, a scroll of white ribbon very graceful in its folds, and shaded with partial transparency.
>
> The detached pieces have a ribbed surface, and a similar scroll re-appears, while for their principal ornament they are dotted with white quatrefoils. These quatrefoils are delicately adjusted in size to the varying circumferences, and are executed both with a true feeling of nature and with a precision that would scarcely discredit a jeweller.[2]

Prince Leopold, like Princess Louise, was asked to a breakfast party at 11, Carlton Hill Terrace, no doubt afterwards being shown the Princess Charlotte déjeuner. Whether he was invited to feel the smoothness of the tray we do not know. Princess Louise and Prince Leopold were the two children of the Queen the Gladstone children came to know best. As sister and brother they were very close, although she was five years older than him. Prince Arthur came between them but he was destined to a career in the army from an early age.

Sir Henry Ponsonby rightly remarked that Leopold was mischievous, and a well-known story circulated how he had teased his nephew, the future Kaiser. It was at the family reunion for the Prince of Wales's wedding, and at the time Leopold was nine and his eldest sister's son was just four. When Leopold saw that his infant nephew's military coatee had tails at the back he thought it absurd.

In next to no time the impulsive young uncle procured scissors and snipped the tails off the coatee. The tiny would-be soldier burst into furious tears, and soon Leopold realised he had gone too far. The tails were sewn back and Leopold not only said he was very sorry but showed such a kindly sparkle in his eyes the two became the best of friends.

Leopold was educated at home with his brothers and sisters, and was allowed to keep caged birds and small dogs as a compensation for having to rest so much. He read a great deal and came to love poetry and music. He was constantly ill and at the age of fifteen his life was in danger, but he pulled through and was soon in his usually high spirits again.

The reader may be wondering how Prince Leopold endured spending so much time resting at Buckingham Palace, but out of the Queen's sight he appears to have chosen to go his own pace. When an undergraduate at Oxford he was given a pony trap to drive himself, which he frequently lent to George Russell who was lame, as Leopold preferred to walk. It was at Oxford that Leopold was to see much of another freshman he already knew and liked, for Herbert was much the same age. Herbert was at University College, whilst Leopold attended Christ Church. He was not allowed by the Queen to reside there but lived with his private tutor, Robert Collins.

Afterwards Herbert stayed on to be a lecturer at Keble College, whilst Leopold became a secretary to the Queen. Within a year of leaving Oxford he nearly died in January 1875. During this illness Robert Collins, his tutor, was always at his bedside.[3] Mary commented in a letter:-

> Prince Leopold's illness seems very serious. It would be so sad if he died, the flower of the flock I believe in intellect and goodness of heart, at all events amongst his brothers . . . .[4]

Leopold recovered and as usual was told to rest. When he was invited to stay in country houses Herbert, being a friend of the same age, was often asked if he would come too. Frequently dates had to be changed when Leopold was not well enough. Both he and Louise were keen Liberals; never missing an opportunity to make their views on the political situation clear to the Gladstone family. Early in 1880 Herbert left Oxford feeling his father's political opinions must be supported, and a few months later became M.P. for Leeds.

In April 1881 a peerage was conferred on Prince Leopold when he was made Duke of Albany. This may be because he had been valuable as a secretary to the Queen, yet the time coincided with his telling her that he very much hoped to get married. The first German princess approached by the Queen would not have him, but the second was Princess Helen of Waldeck and Pyrmont, who made him an ideal wife. She was not wealthy or beautiful in the sense of having perfect features, but highly attractive and able. For the wedding in St. George's Chapel, Windsor, he wore military uniform, but he walked with a pronounced limp caused by his troublesome knee. Mary, who with several members of the family went to the wedding, described it in her diary for April 27th 1882:-

> The procession had such a splendid effect, the flourish of trumpets heralding their approach, the cheering outside, the band and organ within; the gorgeous trains and jewellery and uniforms, the sun shining fitfully; all made a brilliant combination. The Princess of Wales and her three girls dressed all alike in sky blue was the prettiest sight. The bride with downcast head and eyes, led by her father and brother-in-law like a frightened child, the bridesmaids in white with spring flowers. One missed the bridal veil. Prince Leopold looked very nice, flushed and lame. The Archbishop's voice most striking and solemn, the singing and music beautiful.

The new couple, the Duke and Duchess of Albany, lived at Claremont, a beautiful Queen Anne house in Esher, now no more. At the time it was said to be the favourite of the royal residences. In 1883 a daughter was born, Princess Alice; later to be known as Princess Alice, Countess of Athlone, who inherited her father's optimistic outlook on life.

Living in his own house it was no longer practicable for Leopold to continue as secretary to the Queen, and gradually Sir Henry Ponsonby took on his duties.[5] Above all else he now wanted a proper job. He was twenty-nine and had his sights on Canada. His brother-in-law, Lord Lorne, was due to return from his tour of duty in Ottawa as Governor-General. Leopold, before his marriage, had visited Lorne and Louise, and she may have been behind the plan. He must have realised that because of his poor health the odds were heavily stacked against him and that the Queen was unlikely to give her consent, but he evidently wanted the job quite desperately. In his own beautifully formed handwriting he wrote to the Prime Minister pleading that he be given the position:-

Private and Confidential

Windsor Castle,
May 14 '83.

Dear Mr. Gladstone,

I venture to write to take up some of your valuable time in order to bring before you a matter of vital interest to me. You will guess at once that I allude to the Governor-General of Canada and I don't know whether it is quite right to come straight to you like this; but the many years you have known me, and your kindness on various occasions induce me to do so. It has been the one ambition of my life to hold this post, and since I was in Canada three years ago I have most ardently wished for it, and waited the time when Lorne's period of office would expire.

I have during these last three years continued to have conversations with Canadians. When I was there I met all the ministers, as well as several of the opposition and men of all shades of opinion. I tried to get all the information I could about the country, and I have taken an active interest in it ever since. It is the *only* career open to me, by which I can serve my country and the Queen, and I am sure that you will at any rate appreciate my wish. Others, who are distinguished for their parliamentary career, can work for their country politically by becoming Ministers. But one like myself, who from my position am debarred from politics, and who have no active profession of any kind, have *nothing* else open to him.

I know the Cabinet must have good reasons for whoever they appoint, but if, as I still fondly hope, they have not absolutely decided upon Lorne's successor, may I appeal to *you* to help me? I know well that I cannot boast of qualification for the post, such as many distinguished supporters of the Government are possessed of. But I have the welfare of Canada, as well as of this country at heart as much as any Englishman, and no one would be more anxious to work hard, and to strengthen the good feeling between the Dominion and the Mother Country than I am. I would have no fear of difficulties with the Ministers of Canada, as during the last ten years I have constant experience of and insight into Constitutional Government.

But I have taken up enough of your time. I put my case into your hands, dear Mr. Gladstone, with the earnest appeal to you to help me as far as you consider it right to do so.

> Believe me,
> > Yours sincerely,
> > > Leopold.[6]

The letter was, alas, to have a negative result, for he was told that Lord Derby, the Foreign Minister, had already chosen Lord Lorne's successor. It must have been a terrible disappointment but Leopold had infinite courage. A few months later he wrote again pleading for the lesser position as Governor of the Province of British Columbia.

Private

Jan. 3, 1884.

Dear Mr. Gladstone,

I wrote to you last May, before I knew that Lord Lansdowne's appointment to Canada had been finally decided upon, to beg you further, if possible, my desire to go as Governor-General of Canada, and I received a very kind reply from you. But I was too late.

I then made up my mind to wait for another opportunity to ask the Government for Colonial employment. I have heard, only a few days ago, of Lord Normanby's resignation, and I have written to Lord Derby to express my perfect willingness, as well as my strong desire, to go out to Victoria as Governor. I now write to you — and I trust you will excuse me for intruding on your valuable time — to beg of you to recommend my application to Lord Derby. As Prime Minister your wishes on the matter have very great, if not paramount, weight with Lord Derby; and I hope and pray you may feel inclined to further my request. I am so very anxious for active employment, and I have for years past looked to the Colonies as the place or rather object to which I might devote myself, and thus serve my Country.

Hoping that you will look favourably on this letter.

Believe me, dear Mr. Gladstone, with all good wishes for the New Year,

> > Yours sincerely,
> > > Leopold.

I have not yet communicated with the Queen.[7]

Three weeks later the reply arrived. Evidently the Queen had put her foot down.

Downing Street.
Jan. 25, '84.

Sir,

Your Royal Highness will already have learned from Lord Derby the result of the deliberation of the Government on the patriotic desire recently expressed by Your Royal Highness.

I believe, Sir, that you will comprehend even more fully than we can, and will altogether sympathise with Her Majesty's maternal reluctance to a severance at the present moment such as the appointment to the Governorship of Victoria would entail.

Under the circumstances, the Ministers accept the full responsibility of the request that Your Royal Highness's desire may not be further pressed while they have shared the wish so graciously expressed by Her Majesty that a period may arrive when the question may stand clear from any difficulties which for the moment attach to it.

> I have the honour to be, Sir,
> Your Royal Highness's very sincere and faithful servant,
> W. E. Gladstone[8]

Not to be deterred Leopold wrote back almost at once asking to be considered for the post of Governor-General of Australia. It was not to be. On March 3rd he died. He had gone to the south of France to stay with his former equerry, Captain Percival, at Cannes to miss the worst of the winter. He was reported to be in buoyant spirits. Running up a metal spiral staircase at some military barracks they had gone to see he tripped and fell, again damaging his knee. His wife, who was expecting their son, had remained at Claremont. She was only twenty-three. He was thirty.

He was given a splendid funeral. Herbert was there; his father was having one of his minor illnesses and was excused by the Queen. So many royal relations, young and old, arrived from abroad to attend that St. George's Chapel had only one area reserved for distinguished personages, and Herbert must have felt very out of place amongst the elderly and eminent.

As a momento Princess Helen, Duchess of Albany, sent Herbert a gold watch, which she said was the one Leopold had always used. At Oxford members of the Christ Church Society put a marble bust of him, by F. J. Williamson, in the Cathedral, 'in affectionate remembrance.'

12
Mountaineering

The eighteen sixties and seventies are known as the golden age of mountaineering: a golden age when the biggest peaks were climbed for the first time. As young men all four Gladstone sons went out to Switzerland to climb with some remarkable achievements. Few records of holidays were kept but evidently most years they went off discovering new places: the Channel Islands, the Orkney, Shetland and Faroe Islands, Iceland, Norway, Madeira, and the Tirol, only to return to Switzerland again and again. They invariably used the cheapest tickets by steamer and train, and when they had to put up with discomforts it did not occur to them to complain, for within their lifetime travel through central Europe had become immeasurably easier. The new linkwork of railways made Switzerland readily accessible and the Alps, looked upon in the eighteenth century as an ugly barrier, became recognised in the nineteenth for their beauty and grandeur.

The British cherished Switzerland. They found the air exhilarating, and the alpine meadows and snowy peaks a welcome change from their own environment. They flocked there in ever-increasing numbers, and in 1871 Leslie Stephen titled his book on climbing in Switzerland, with a hint of sarcasm, '*The Playground of Europe.*'

The season for mountaineering lasted from the end of June till the beginning of October, but good weather could, of course, never be relied on. In 1873 all four brothers went to the Bernese Oberland: Stephy and Herbert in July, and Willy and Harry in September. At the time Stephy was working as a clergyman in Lambeth, then one of the poorest and roughest areas in London. After some expeditions he had to return, leaving Herbert who was an undergraduate at Oxford and had stayed on to read, a chance to attempt the Jungfrau, or more likely reach the less formidable Jungfraujoch.

The weather seeming good Herbert set off with two friends, one of the well-established local guides to whom the British owed all their climbing feats, and a porter, whom he described as a 'phantod,' which in family language meant an apparition. The party relied on advice from the guide since there were no detailed maps, and the porter carried the food. One, or both, carried a brandy flask.

They had been staying at the Jungfrau Hotel at the foot of the Eggishorn and south of the Jungfraujoch, and first set off in the afternoon to climb for three and a half hours to reach the Faulberg hut. This was a cave-like shelter with

six bunk beds and room for little else, and was renowned amongst the British for its discomfort, although Herbert remarked that having five sleepers was not as bad as having six. For so cramped was the space that the person nearest the entrance, a position usually taken by the guide, could not open the door without moving the bunks, whilst the others could not escape the snores and stuffiness without clambering over each other.

> It was the funniest thing in the world going to bed — all in a row with handkerchiefs for nightcaps. We got up after (of course) scarcely any sleep at 1.15, and after breakfast started at 2.00 exactly. The night was very dark and fine, and the fact of having failed to bring a lantern caused us to start slowly (roped) as the glacier was full of big crevasses.[1]

Except for their hats, which were replaced with handkerchiefs knotted at the corners, they slept in their clothes. All wore coats coming down to cover the hips, either breeches or trousers, gaiters, and boots studded with nails. It was necessary to be prepared for frosty nights but also for a burning sun by day. An essential item was a hat with a big brim to guard against sunburn from which the British suffered especially severely in mid-summer, they often resorted to dark glasses, veils or masks. The men all had alpenstocks, sticks as tall as themselves with a steel point at the tip and sometimes a metal bar across the top or a decorative carving.

Roped together and with the guide leading them the party of five slowly made their way to a plateau, then known as the Place de la Concorde, to see by the pink blush of the first sunlight the breathtaking view of the serrated horizon. Then steadily progressing they found themselves at the Jungfraujoch, at the base of the gigantic Jungfrau, by 4.30. It was vital to attempt the ascent to the summit whilst the snow was still firm, and they remained roped all the time. Herbert felt he did not have a good head for heights, but this adventure seems to prove that this was not true.

> We reached the foot of the Jungfrau at about 4.30. First came a small and steep snow slope with a bridge over a crevasse. Then some very steep rock climbing — so steep to us that we had to give up our alpenstocks to the guide to use both hands. After this some long snow slopes in which the guide very kindly cut steps though not positively necessary. It was beautiful to see him, he did it so clearly and regularly. After rather more than an hour of this we came to the steepest slope of all. We first crossed a crevasse by a snow bridge, then up the slope above which was an overhanging edge of snow. The guide took us up with great care and rapidity. Then cutting a hole through the cornice of snow he passed through and I followed him.

To facilitate the steeper areas the guide cut steps, and to climb the sheer faces he offered his shoulders as a ladder: the most proficient of the party going first and throwing a rope down to pull up the others. The sight of the rocky pyramidal edge together with the change of altitude was terrifying, and here the brandy was passed around. Herbert described the next stage:-

> I found myself on an arête, and quite unexpectedly a most extraordinarily lovely view burst

upon us of mountains and valleys towards the west, with a precipice immediately beneath us as we stood in amazement. We had now got past what the guide called the 'mauvais pas' and all that remained was a long continuous climb up steep slopes of snow varied with rocks overhanging and a precipice. Mr. Copleston here became rather faint, and he almost despaired of reaching the top. However, by stopping frequently and nips of brandy he succeeded in doing so. The top is a most wonderful place and here I felt a little bit nervous. It is an arête with a precipice on each side, quite the worst sort of place for a giddy person. We walked along this till we reached the highest point, then I sat down with a leg dangling down each precipice; of course, not absolutely sheer, but nearly so. The view was indeed magnificent. I was prepared for a fine sight but was absolutely amazed at its grandeur. The whole of Switzerland and more, seemed laid at our feet . . . .

They spent a mere quarter of an hour at the summit, as Herbert explained, 'as it is very cold sitting astride of ice!' It was still only nine o'clock in the morning, and the descent was estimated to take seven hours. They had been very fortunate as the view is often lost in thick cloud.

As they proceeded downwards the snow became more and more slushy. It was just as well the ropes stayed on as at one place Mr. Copleston sunk into a crevice up to his shoulders and had to be gently hauled out. There was also the danger of the sun bringing snow and rocks down, and at one stage the guide screamed 'avalanche' and, tiredness forgotten, they ran 150 metres. They stopped for some food and short rests but the lower slopes meant climbing through snow up to their knees and sometimes to their hips.

The notion of spending another night at the Faulberg hut was an experience they thought they could do without, and they continued down. Crossing the Aletsch glacier in soft snow Herbert commented:-

In coming over the glacier I went through the snow up to my middle in a crevasse of no great width, but was held up directly by the rope. We were roped for thirteen hours consecutively and heartily glad I was to be free again.

Then finally small trees and wooden buildings with vast stones on the roofs came into view and at last they reached the hotel, glad to have survived and too tired (or, as Herbert put it 'rather done up') to worry. Later, unable to explain how he had managed the ascent, he cheerfully reflected: 'it must have been the excitement that kept off the fatigue!'

The Eiger, although less high than the Jungfrau, is a much more dangerous mountain. The Jungfrau had been first climbed in 1811, the Eiger in 1858. Willy and Harry, then respectively thirty-two and twenty-two, had been climbing from Zermatt and Chamonix before they attempted the Eiger on 30th September. By this time Willy was a very experienced climber who appears to have been as good as the best, never missing his annual holiday in the Swiss Alps. Perhaps he kept quiet on these exploits so as not to worry his parents. yet the standard reply as to the dangers of mountaineering was that the chances of an accident on a railway in England was much more probable, and a glance at the newspapers of the time tells us how numerous these were.

As Willy commented they made 'a very brief but vigorous raid on the Oberland!' Afterwards Harry asked his elder brother to write an account of the memorable day for him, for the mere thought of the adventure made him writhe. The challenge of the Eiger had already been discussed with Hans Baumann, one of the pre-eminent guides of the period. Feeling the weather was set fine they took the train to Interlaken, already a resort with a row of hotels, and British tourists grumbling over the high price of a ham sandwich. With the mountain range well in view, they stopped at the post office to send a telegram to Baumann. They hired a horse and cart to take them through pretty scenery to reach the glacier village of Grindelwald, the excitement of the Eiger on their minds.

Arriving at Grindelwald they found Baumann waiting outside the Adler Hotel and Willy, in his usual unassuming way, asked him in German if he thought the Eiger was practicable. Plans of precautions were exchanged but there was no delay or fuss, and after some lunch they walked the 10 km. to the Wengen Alp Inn, where they were to spend the night in preparation.

They took with them two guides, Hans Baumann and Peter Kaufmann, a younger man. An early start was essential and soon after four they crossed the meadows to start climbing on snow. Already there were patches of shingle, which was to turn out to be their chief difficulty. By the time they had reached the foot of the mountain daylight had broken.

> At 6 we had attained a good height and paused a few minutes at a spot on the N.W. ridge to put on the rope: Baumann first, then I, then Kaufmann, and Harry last. The climb then became stiffer, and it was a relief when we were able to utilise patches of snow which were, however, steep and hard, and required a little care.
>
> At 7 we rested for breakfast, again at a point on the edge of the mountain, with terrific precipices close at hand. Here the guides conversed together as to the route to be followed, as they observed that the rocks above were coated with ice. These, however, they contrived to avoid, and we wound rather rapidly upwards by a tortuous way keeping generally some little way from the ridge.[2]

From where they stood the summit of the Monch did not seem far though in reality it was more than a kilometre away beyond the spur of the Eiger. There is no easy route to the Eiger summit. It is severe in character and much of the climbing is over shingle which may fall loose. Continuing the steady grind they stopped at 9.30 to have a half-hour rest and review the way they would attempt the final ascent. Although the top appeared very near Baumann warned them that it would take at least two hours to get there. He then pointed out that if they took the more usual route on the main snow slope it would be necessary to cut steps the whole way and this would take too long, for it was essential not to leave the descent until too late. It was after all the last day of September. Willy continued his narrative:-

We therefore went straight up the rocks along the ridge and close to the edge. Baumann now led up a sort of 'chimney' which soon became extremely steep and the holding very treacherous. He seemed for the moment perturbed and uneasy . . . . Every stone here had to be tested before it could be trusted and the progress was slow, one moving at a time as far as practicable.

They were frightened not only of slipping but of setting off an avalanche from above. Just at this crucial stage Harry let go his alpenstock, and in less than no time it had shot down the icy mountainside never to be seen again. As a result, when he reached the final slope Harry said he would not go on. The guides conferred and then insisted, encouraging him by cutting excellent steps. Even Willy admitted:-

Still, I will own I was glad to have my own axe, for the slope was very rapid, and we were within 2 feet of the edge overhanging the dizziest of precipices, and treading on the very border of the snow cornice. The ice was very hard at first — afterwards slightly less so — but good steps (the guides relieving each other) were necessary to the very summit.

So the final testing steps were taken, but at times they felt they were making almost no progress as they measured their height against rocky promontories. The last hour and a half were the most tedious when time appeared to be going very slowly, but:-

At last the form of the mountain contracted before us, and we could see the apex in which the three ridges culminate. Suddenly, we see the 'cairn' in the shape of a bottle stuck into the aforesaid apex, and our magnificent staircase of 200 steps lands us at the goal of our hopes and ambitions, and renders us masters of the Eiger and all he commands . . . .

Reaching the top Baumann waved his hat and yodelled to celebrate. The forty minutes they stayed seemed to pass in a flash, as they rested and contemplated the view.

The descent was to prove even more treacherous. Here the order was changed with young Peter Kaufmann leading, then Harry, then Willy and finally Baumann. As if to show an air of confidence Kaufmann lit up his pipe and then offering Harry a helping hand they proceeded downwards, manipulating one step at a time. All the while Baumann and Willy anchored themselves with their ice axes, and Baumann called out 'ganz fest' before the lower two moved. They kept going as fast as possible, yet with infinite carefulness; and, their limbs aching, they were thankful to stop at the breakfast place where a bottle of wine had been left. They had already quenched their thirst with wine on the way up, and now fortified with more they continued in a lighthearted spirit. Later, time was saved with a sort of glissade over old snow, which proved very rough.

At six they took off the rope, and dusk was falling as they reached the Wengen Alp Inn. The expedition had taken fourteen hours and both were ecstatic at having reached the top. Harry admitted that if he had known 'that was the way up he could not have had the hardihood to go,' whilst Willy, a fearless climber,[3] noted that the memory would be 'cherished with a lively pleasure,' for he ended his report on their ascent of the Eiger:-

> From some points of view — Mürren, for example — the face of the mountain appears unassailable, yet it will appear from what I have said that in favourable weather and with good guides the ascent of the Eiger is free from danger, while it is certainly attended with the greatest interest, and will be cherished with the most lively pleasure.

Two years before Willy had returned from Switzerland with a huge St. Bernard puppy he called Alp. The boys each had their own dogs. With names like Phyllis, Tip, Charlie and Dandy, they included spaniels and terriers, but at Hawarden the gamekeeper, Hurst, sometimes looked after them. The girls did not have their own dogs and it seems that Agnes, at any rate, had mixed feelings about them for when Willy turned up with Alp she noted in a letter:-

> The news is the arrival of the St. Bernard puppy, a regular baby about Phyllis's size, with a very disproportionate head and paws. He is blackish grey colour, very shy and awkward, cannot well scramble up and down steps but licks one's hands and takes refuge about legs and petticoats. I regret to say that the odour about him is not savoury or sweet.

The Lyttelton cousins had been brought up on cricket. Willy had won the School Fives competition at Eton, but in the main the Gladstones preferred less competitive pastimes. They preferred walking and climbing, and then there was the occasional tree cutting. Generally their father would enlist help, and sometimes he and all four boys would work with their axes at the same tree, as they hewed chips from the base. There was great excitement when the tree was about to fall and everybody was collected to come and watch. Once Harry, then about thirteen, was fixing a rope to the top of a partly cut tree so as to direct the fall, when it began to snap as the inside was rotten. Only because he quickly swivelled his body round to land on top of the trunk did he survive, bruised and badly shaken.

As for Agnes, Mary and Helen, they did not go abroad so often and certainly did not go off in pairs, because the conventions of the time were so constricting. Gradually customs were becoming more relaxed and Helen was to the fore in gaining independence. In 1883 when she was working as Secretary at Newnham College, Cambridge, she and Herbert spent some of the summer vacation climbing in Switzerland, much to her joy.

13

The Gentle Brethren

The two uncles the family came to know best were Stephen and Henry Glynne who, it will be remembered, were known in North Wales as 'the gentle brethren,' being unassuming in manner, calm and unselfish, and much loved by the Welsh. As the Gladstone and Lyttelton children grew up they would question their fathers, the two great scholars, on all manner of subjects: geography, history, literature, religion and politics. Now occasionally, but increasingly as the questions became more complex the fathers differed in their replies. What then to do? Why, turn to Uncle Stephen, who with his great fund of knowledge would invariably give them the answer that proved to be the correct one.[1]

'Our dear Uncle was more like a father than anything else,' noted Harry in his diary, for Uncle Stephen made himself available to listen though he never gave advice unless asked. As the children grew to adulthood they would sometimes stay up chatting late, enjoying games, or playing the piano and singing part-songs, and when he felt it was time for bed he would say nothing, but simply snuff out the candles until the voices quietened and they disappeared. Once, Arthur Balfour, staying as a guest, relit the candles with a smile, but realising that this was being frowned upon he extinguished them himself.

Uncle Stephen did not marry. Uncle Harry (as they knew the Rector) married George Lyttelton's younger sister, Lavinia, in St. George's, Hanover Square, in 1842. They lived in a huge rectory at Hawarden, having taken over from George Neville Grenville, who had twelve children. It was not uncommon for children to die early, but Henry and Lavinia had a tragic sequence of deaths. They lost a son and two daughters; then another daughter in childhood, and in 1850 after the arrival of Gertrude, their only child to survive, Lavinia had become so delicate she died.

On Tuesday, July 30th 1872, Henry as rural dean rode some fifteen miles to inspect a church at Gwernaffield, which had been rebuilt. He was caught in a violent thunderstorm, but whether he was struck by lightening there is some uncertainty. To avoid the torrential rain he stopped at Rhual Hall and called on Captain Phillips, the High Sheriff of Flintshire, having sheltered in the stables where he left his horse. He then inspected the church he had come to see and returned to Captain Phillips, who repeatedly offered his carriage to the clergyman who had been soaked to the skin by the heavy rain.

Returning home to his only child, Gertrude, then aged eleven, he declined dinner and went to bed. Later, but too late, the village doctor, Dr. Moffat, was called and 'ordered stimulants to restore animation, every effort proving of no avail.' The man who had been Uncle Harry to the many Gladstone and Lyttelton children died during the night. He was sixty-two. His sudden death shocked the village, and on the Sunday the curate preached from the same text[2] as had been used following President Lincoln's recent assassination in Philadelphia, likening the two events as 'so overwhelming a calamity.'

The funeral took place on Monday, August 5th, with some three to four thousand people[3] gathering from the surrounding villages. A large procession lined up, first the men in fours and then the women in fours, followed by the schoolchildren. Although it was August the choirboys wore gloves as a sign of mourning and the men of the choir wore gloves and scarves. Then came the two village doctors followed by several clergy. The church had been decorated with violet velvet and white silk crosses with white geraniums, and in the address it was said of the gentle Rector:-

> He was not a man whose career had been marked by any great vicissitude; on the contrary, he contented himself with an ever quiet life, doing good among his fellow-men and women without noise or parade, looking only to his own conscience and to Him that seeth in *secret* for his reward.

The village of Hawarden was not without its intellectuals: in particular, Dr. Moffat, the doctor and surgeon who had been trained in Scotland. He was always dressed entirely in black and, out of doors, would wear a tall top hat, befitting his profession. He spent his life working in the village except when he was away attending learned societies, for he was a fellow of the Royal Astronomical Society and Geological Society, and a member of the British Meteorological Society. He lectured all over Britain, often publishing papers; on potato disease, the theory of earthquakes, atmospheric ozone, and many other scientific subjects of a practical nature.

Stephen Glynne chose the nephew who had been named after him as the new Rector of Hawarden. Stephy Gladstone was twenty-eight at the time. Of the same age was his first cousin, Albert Lyttelton (both being second sons were destined for the church) who joined him as a curate, and provided a mirthful diversion in the neighbourhood as the archetypal absent-minded clergyman.

Albert had been named after his godfather, the Prince Consort. He was put in charge of the newly-built church of Pentrobin. Whereas Stephy soon became recognised for being capable and well-organised, Albert was hopelessly vague and very fond of a casual chat. As a result stories of his vagueness became legendary. He sadly lacked tact. At funerals Albert would welcome relations, squeezing his hands together and cheerfully announce: 'Here we are again!'

As bicycles came on the scene he would use one to get around the parish, dismounting when he met a familiar face to pass the time of day. At one crossroads after an absorbing discussion he had to ask for assistance. 'Tell me, which direction did I come from?' he asked the astounded listener, and when informed rejoined: 'Ah, thanks; must have had lunch.'

Another story portrays Albert on a blustery evening tricycling to attend a parish meeting. His light blew out and he had great difficulty relighting it in the face of an oncoming wind. He finally turned his tricycle round, and managed to keep a match burning long enough to relight his lamp. However, he never turned up at the meeting, for he had turned his machine towards home, where he soon arrived back having forgotten all about the meeting he had set out to attend.

Stephy would occasionally discuss Parish problems with his father. A clergyman's decision on who may marry in church is as difficult as any he has to take. Stephy was caught in this dilemma when a loyal parishioner, whose wife had died, wished to marry a local widow. The two had lived together for some time causing great disruption in the village when the banns were called. After much reflection Stephy recommended that the couple should be married in a registry office and they would then be welcomed to attend church. He had discussed the problem with his father at great length and wrote to him:-

> . . . . So it is settled. I feel it is a tremendously responsible step to take: but under the circumstances it seemed the best thing, and I had the strongest feelings against the banns being given again tomorrow. We shall take special care to try and befriend him after a decent interval.

It was Stephen Glynne who termed the phrase 'the great people' for William and Catherine, who were often referred to within the family as the G.P.s. William had first made friends with Stephen at Eton and Christ Church, Oxford. Until he was forty he was a Member of Parliament representing the locality he lived in. Having lost an election 1847 he ceased to live in London and lived at Hawarden most of the year, where he was a magistrate and Lord-Lieutenant of Flintshire.

Some people's interests and recreations are extravagant whereas others derive their pleasure with virtually no expenditure. From an early age Stephen Glynne became fascinated with the architecture and history of medieval churches. It was an intriguing occupation, for no two churches are the same, and every year it took him to new areas of the country. By the time of his death he had visited and made notes on over five and a half thousand of them, and his accumulation of knowledge made him an expert. He made copious notes surveying the churches and noting details of the churchyards.[4] These are of special value because the observations were made before so many churches had extensive Victorian restorations. He joined the Institute of Archaeology and always attended meetings. To get to lonely parishes he went by train whenever possible and then hired a horse. He took his servant Alfred with him to help with clothes and luggage which tended to be heavy, though in mid-Victorian times a gentleman who took only one servant was classified as travelling alone. He always enjoyed visiting the vicar and exchanging views, and would find himself invited to stay in houses large and small.

A guest whose unruffled temper, constant readiness to be pleased, calm cheerfulness and unvarying kindness, joined in his vast stores of information, ever made his visits more welcome.

Like his brother, Stephen died peacefully but suddenly. On June 17th 1874, he had been visiting Suffolk to look at churches and returned by train to London, arriving at Shoreditch station where he left a small leather bag and a hatbox at the left luggage office. Shortly after he collapsed, and a man called Alfred Sweeny went to his aid.

Alfred Sweeny said he was a labourer and was occasionally employed as a shoeblack. On Wednesday morning last, about half past ten, he was standing near the corner of Silver Street, Shoreditch, when he noticed a large crowd of working men. Upon getting up to see whatever was the matter he saw the deceased lying on the pavement apparently very ill. Deceased asked witness to procure a glass of water, which he did. Afterwards he was asked by deceased to assist him into a doctor's shop close by. Witness then assisted into the shop of Dr. Flack in High Street, Shoreditch, and there left him.

Stephen Glynne died on the doctor's sofa at the back of the shop. True to the last he was unobtrusive, and only reluctantly did he give his name and explained that he was about to visit his niece, Agnes Wickham, at Wellington College.

In 1875 the house at 11 Carlton House Terrace and most of its contents including all the valuable pictures and china were sold, and a house was rented at 73, Harley Street. The family had been installed in Stephen Glynne's house at Hawarden since the 1850's as a consequence of the Oak Farm financial crisis, the result of a speculative venture on Glynne property in Staffordshire, which so greatly reduced his income that he could not afford to keep up his big house. With the help of his brother-in-law he was able to do so, and it was said that this troublesome experience had led him to be such a successful Chancellor of the Exchequer. Stephen and William both continued to live in the house entirely amicably: the former always sitting at the head of the table but referring to the Gladstones as the 'great people.' It had been agreed that after Stephen's death the house and estate would belong to Willy.

Visitors evermore flocked to the park to get a view of the famous statesman, for this was a time before photographs appeared in newspapers. For example Herbert preserved a cutting from the *Tyldesley Journal* which, as clown of the family, particularly amused him. On August 19th 1876 a party of 600 Liberals from Leigh and Tyldesley, small industrial towns west of Manchester, arrived on a special excursion train. Despite rain 'excellent good humour prevailed and bon mots were the order of the day.' In a steady downpour the men walked from Queensferry the two miles uphill to reach Hawarden, and as they entered the grounds Catherine heard the band they had brought with them. By the time she had fetched her husband the crowd was interspersed with a large number of cows that had also been attracted by the band.

'Had you to walk up from Queensferry?' asked Mr. Gladstone, apparently unperturbed at having to address cows as well as the motley crowd.

'Yes,' was the answer, and a voice called out, 'It was wetter than we liked.'

However, by then the weather had cleared, and the excursionists decided they had enjoyed themselves so much on their day in the Welsh countryside that it was agreed the tour would become an annual event.

14

Weddings

By 1871 the family had pretty well grown up. Willy was thirty and Herbert was seventeen. Their parents were living at 10 Downing Street, but had kept on their house at 11 Carlton House Terrace. March 29th 1871, was a day to remember when Papa and the five living in London delighted in attending the opening ceremony at the Royal Albert Hall, sitting in the box reserved for government ministers in the grand tier. Catherine chose not to go. Helen was at an educational establishment in Dorset, which included hunting which she loathed, as one of its forms of passing the time for young ladies. Herbert was still at Eton College, as were the four youngest Lyttelton boys.

In 1869 their widowed father, George married Sybella, the widow of Humphrey Mildmay, M.P. It was twelve years since Mary, Catherine's sister, by whom he had his twelve children, had died. The two eldest of the family, Meriel and Lucy, were now married, and probably the engagement came as no surprise to the elder children who had noticed their father's admiration for Mrs. Mildmay. However, apparently nobody thought to prepare the youngest four boys who were still at school for this great change which seemed 'strange and rather dreadful.' The eldest of the four, Arthur, then seventeen, wrote to his cousin Mary Gladstone, then twenty-one, pouring out his heart at this news which he resolved to 'look forward to with honour.'

Eton College,
May 9, 1869.

Dear Mary,

I thought I would not answer you letter till today as I was under the impression that Papa was going to bring her down here yesterday. But he could not come, so my delay was no good.

I am recovering a little from the hurly-burly I was in when I first heard of the great change, and I am getting more and more to accustom myself to it. Of course there will be intense I don't know what to call it of next holidays, when everything will seem strange and rather dreadful. This I look forward to with honour. But the advantages and the comfort it will be to Papa are enormous, and outweigh every other consideration, I think.

It must have been startling to you, unless you have been prepared for it, or had guessed it. As for me it knocked me down very nearly, and made as unhappy as possible at first . . . .

Your affect. coz.
Arthur Lyttelton.[1]

Arthur duly became Principal of Selwyn College, Cambridge, at a very early age, and later a bishop. It cannot have been at all easy for

Sybella Mildmay to have inherited twelve stepchildren, and Lucy describes 'the desperate stiffness and shyness of all parties' at the first meeting. The marriage was a very quiet affair and in due course three more Lyttelton daughters were born.

Everything was not so quiet for the Gladstones who did not always enjoy the fame of their father. In 1870 Herbert was confirmed at St. John's Church, Brixton, in a far from peaceful ceremony, when the Bishop preached for the liquidation of the building debt.[2] To draw attention to the church's need for funds William and Catherine had been invited to attend. As a result the church was packed. Herbert together with Mary and Helen and their parents sat in a front pew, whilst persons at the back made a clatter standing on pews in an effort to get a better view, so that the verger had to plead for quiet in the house of God.

After leaving Eton Willy and Stephy had been to Oxford University. Harry had not the same scholastic ability but Stephy felt he should be given the same chance. Stephy knew the only way he could put his reasons for Harry going to Oxford to his father was to write a letter, and in a forthright manner he made clear his feelings:-

98 Upper Kennington Lane, S.E.
Oct. 6, '69

My dear Papa,

I rather gather from Mama's letter that it is settled against Harry's going to Oxford at all, but I should like to give my share of advice in case the matter is still open . . . .

The variety of associations one *cannot* fail to acquire at the University . . . . make me hope that if you determine not to send him to Oxford, you will have strong reasons for the choice. A great friend of mine . . . . tells me that it is only advisable to go straight from school to the office in the case of those who have no prospects of partnership. Such as these must begin very early and steadily work their way up by *long* assiduity. He also says that the University is dangerous in the case of those who are ordered to go into business, as they may be spoilt for it. But my idea is that Harry, having fairly chosen his profession, would not be in due danger of being spoilt for hard work by the pleasure he would derive from lots of spare time at Oxford . . . .

Your affectionate son,
S. E. Gladstone.[3]

The letter, not the only one of this sort sent to their father, was brushed aside, and Harry attended King's College, London, for a couple of years. He lived with Stephy. They boarded at 98, Upper Kennington Lane, in a house which still stands. Stephy, who was ordained in March 1870, worked as a curate at St. Mary-the-Less, Lambeth, and walking home late in the evening would carry an umbrella to protect himself from interfering drunks, a multi-purpose weapon either to poke them off or to hide behind. Harry's first job was to work in the city at James Wyllie and Co. as an unpaid clerk. To save money he would go by bus in one direction and walk the other. It was an era when the ridden horse was fast disappearing from the London scene and the vast majority of people walked to work. A bus ride costing a halfpenny was a considerable expense to him and he chose to avoid the busiest bridges which pedestrians had to pay a toll to cross.

Frequently Stephy and Harry would call to see their parents at 10, Downing Street, often for breakfast or dinner. Both loathed grand parties, but particularly Harry, who refused to attend balls after one at the Cavendish Bentincks, when he felt he was literally being suffocated by the crush of the smart people, while the small talk and gossip did little to revive him. This was still the period of the great London houses, 'when the balls at Grosvenor House were a party; the balls at Stafford House a mob.' With tail coats flying and ladies dresses with swinging trains, the company would waltz away until dawn. In Downing Street where there were formal dinners and grand receptions the domestic staff apparently sympathised with Harry's fear of mixing in the mêlée, and a kind maid would bring him an ice cream to eat on the servants' landing on the top floor!

In 1873 Stephy left Lambeth to become Rector of Hawarden following the sudden death of his uncle, Henry Glynne, and Harry went to India to join a business in 1874. Two years later Stephy again wrote to his father saying he, too, would like to go to India to work as a missionary. He never went. It was an accepted convention that 'elders were betters' and that parents' views should be honoured.

The first of the Gladstone family to be married was Agnes. She was very beautiful with refined features and of rather more conventional tastes than her two younger sisters, which was perhaps just as well as she married a young headmaster, the Reverend Edward Wickham, Principal of Wellington College. After the ceremony in Hawarden Church the villagers were offered tea for all, and in the evening a dance in the new girls' school was run by Catherine and Willy, when the loving cup was passed around. Amongst the numerous presents the Queen gave an Indian shawl, Baroness Burdett Coutts a china and gold clock, and the boys of Wellington College generously gave silver desert knives, forks and spoons.[4] For their honeymoon the couple spent several weeks visiting some of the largest and most aristocratic houses in the country, when Agnes kept a visitors' book.

Then there was the sensitive question of what Edward should call his father and mother-in-law. Instead of calling them by their surnames, which they apparently expected, he called them Papa and Mama, and when he and Agnes stayed the next Christmas the family 'became quite desperate for he did it every second.'[5] After fearful consultation with the Lyttelton girls, Mary decided to write to Agnes asking her to correct Edward and hoping they would not be offended. They were not.

Two years later, in 1875, Willy married. There had been some talk that he might marry his cousin, Gertrude Glynne. In 1873 we hear of them going by train together from Queensferry to Penmaenmawr, where a seaside house was rented. They went off together, but hardly alone, for Willy took Alp, Dandy, and Moss on this holiday. Gertrude, who was very dainty and an excellent dancer, may have found the dogs got most attention.

By this time Willy had already established a habit of going off on holidays by himself. He seldom accepted invitations from country houses, and seems to have had a need to get away from his parents. Since 1868 he had represented Whitby in North Yorkshire, and was a conscientious Member of Parliament. He had been a junior whip, and like Stephy and Harry lived in lodgings in London. During the social season of 1875 he became engaged to Gertrude Stuart, whose parents owned 41, Berkeley Square. Gerty, as she was known, was the fourth and youngest daughter of Lord and Lady Blantyre, whose country home was Erskine House, Glasgow. Lord Blantyre was a knowledgeable and innovative agriculturalist.[6] Lady Blantyre, Evelyn, was the second daughter of the Duke and Duchess of Sutherland. Gerty had, on her mother's side, three aunts who were all Duchesses — Elizabeth, Duchess of Argyle; Caroline, Duchess of Leinster; and Constance, Duchess of Westminster.

Several years previously Willy had proposed to Gerty's elder sister, Mary Stuart, and not been given any encouragement. All the family took to Gerty, and Mary commented of her future sister-in-law:-

> Mr. Shaw-Stewart calls her far the brightest, pleasantest, nicest, and most pliable of the lot. (You know they have rather a name for obstinacy.) Alas, we hear from behind the scenes from her great friend, Lily Labouchère, that she really cared for Willy the season before last, and that since her engagement to him it has been a joke in the family . . . .

The wedding was in London with Charles Lyttelton as best man, and six bridesmaids dressed in palest blue, including Mary and Helen. The Queen gave a magnificent Cashmere shawl, and the Prince of Wales sent a valuable travelling clock[7] with 'such a pretty letter' the night before the wedding. Later the happy couple were welcomed at Hawarden, where Willy now owned the house and the estate following the death of his uncle, Stephen Glynne, though his parents were to live there during their life-time. Lucy Cavendish (Lyttelton) described the scene in her diary:-

> The carriages, drawn by men from the top of the village, and surrounded and pursued by cheers, came opposite us in due course, and it would be hard to say which of the two beaming faces were most good to look at . . . . I always did think Willy's face beautiful, especially with his bright embellishing smile; and she! She's a fair noble creature that all Hawarden will be proud of.

And as for Gertrude Glynne, who had been accompanied by Willy's three dogs when she went with him to the seaside, her wedding was three weeks after his. She married the Honourable George Douglas Pennant, heir to Lord Penrhyn, and duly had a large family from which there are many descendants.

15
Schlüter

Before we left Dublin this morning I went with Mrs. Gladstone to the photographers. Such fun, the photographer kept on saying to Mrs. Gladstone: 'Open your eyes and shut your mouth,' until Madam and I burst into peals of laughter and he turned quite cross. He did not seem to realise that Mrs. Gladstone's lips were always apart. Well, to my joy, Mrs. Gladstone told the man to take me, her young friend, as she called me.[1]

Who was Catherine's young friend? It was her ladies maid, Auguste Schlüter. They were in Dublin with time to spare, and Catherine knew that it would give pleasure to her maid to have her photograph taken, which she could send back to her family in Germany.

Auguste Schlüter had come over from Hanover at the age of seventeen in 1867, and originally joined the family because they needed a chaperon for Mary and Helen. Everywhere they went in London young women had to be accompanied. London a century ago was a rough place, although the chaperon fulfilled a duty that was a social rather than a practical necessity. Schlüter was younger than Mary and Helen. She was employed as their ladies maid and helped with their clothes, doing the necessary repairs and alterations, and packing and selecting for she also like to offer her advice as to what they should wear. She would help with their hair for special occasions avoiding the need for a hairdresser to come to the house, but the reason for having her was first and foremost to serve as a companion. She would accompany them in the daytime when they wanted to visit friends or go shopping, or simply for walks, and go with them to concerts and plays. She adored her ladies and, as she said: 'I am always lonely without my ladies.'

She thought Catherine was wonderful, and William could do no wrong. She soon became attached to the family and the family attached to her. She was never happier than with Harry and Herbert. A particularly hilarious day was spent when her sister came from Germany, and they went with the two H's, as they were called, to Madame Tussaud's waxworks. Schlüter had a soft spot for Herbert, being the youngest of the family, and her story, most often repeated, was about him. 'Have you heart about Mr. Herbert and the pram?' she would commence.

Herbert had been down to the local station at Broughton, near Hawarden, in the dogcart to pick up a parcel, when he saw a woman pushing a pram full of luggage with a small child pulling at her skirt. He felt sorry for her and politely asked if she would like to get into the trap. The dogcart was a small two-wheeled cart with seats back-to-back pulled by a pony. No sooner was the offer made than the woman was in the cart and the pony trotting off at a brisk pace, leaving him to push the pram. To his consternation he saw that under sacks of food was a baby. Horrified at being left behind, he later told Schlüter, he never stopped running the two miles all the way uphill to Hawarden. He hardly managed to run with the ramshackle pram to keep in view of the dogcart and pony who was heading homewards.

After the London house at 11, Carlton House Terrace was sold, the family rented 73, Harley Street, which became their London home until they were back in Downing Street. On Sunday, February 12th 1878, William and Catherine were out and Mary and Schlüter were spending an evening at home in this pleasant house in Harley Street when, to their horror, they heard a noisy crowd in front of the house shouting abuse. Schlüter noted in her diary:-

> About five o'clock this afternoon a dreadful crowd of people came to our door, groaning and lifting their fists towards our windows wanting war. I am happy to say our Gentleman was out and only Miss Mary and I at home. It all sounded very awful, but nothing happened as our door was guarded by sixteen police.

On the following Sunday she noted:-

> . . . . tremendous crowds at our door again. This time they even smashed our windows. Then about sixty police drove the people off and guarded our house till all turned quiet.[2]

The rowdiness and violence were protests against William's attitude to the Russo-Turkish war. Disraeli, misled by an incompetent ambassador, had belittled Turkish atrocities against the Christian Bulgarians. The Turkish government had used the Bashi-Bazouks, irregular troops, to suppress a Bulgarian rising, and the resultant massacres (12,000 Christian perished in one district) were accompanied by pillage, rape and torture. William thereupon wrote his famous pamphlet, *The Bulgarian Horrors and the Question of the East*, which sold 40,000 copies in less than a week, made a great open-air speech at Blackheath and appealed to the humanity of his audiences at many great meetings. However, many of the British public still had a strong hatred of Russia, and Russia was at war with Turkey. It seemed for some months that Disraeli might lead the country to side with the Turks, and it was this jingo fever, or jingoism, which motivated the crowds in Harley Street. As the music hall song ran:-

> We don't want to fight, but by jingo if we do,
> We've got the ships, we've got the men, we've got the money too.

William and Catherine decided to accept the invitation to move temporarily to a friend's house, and hoped the animosity would subside in a few weeks. As they left through the front door, the closely-knit crowd was unaware of them. Suddenly the big door opened, the gentleman lifted his hat, and an elderly couple were disappearing down Harley Street.

To the surprise of everyone, in the full tide of the tumult, the Gladstone's front door opened, and out walked the old couple, arm-in-arm, and passed right into the midst of the very people who had been hurling stones through their windows. With the grand manner of an old courtier the statesman took off his hat, made a profound bow to the populace, and before the mob had recovered from its astonishment, he had walked away down the street with his wife.[3]

Two years later the Liberals were victorious, and William became Prime Minister for the second time. Schlüter found the uncertainty almost unbearable for elections continued for more than a week after the result became clear, and admitted to giving away to her emotions with a few tears. Returning to Downing Street meant much to her and she noted the sequence of events in her diary:-

This week has been one of the most exciting ones in my life. Within a few days our gentleman was made the first in the land. Last Monday he returned, and Mr. Henry the same time from Calcutta. Very anxious days followed the Monday, as the Queen could not make up her mind. Everybody became very excited, then she sent for Lord Hartington on Thursday. In the evening nothing was settled: it was almost too much for me! On Friday Lord Granville was sent for, and he and Lord Hartington rode back to Windsor.

I went out for the house felt stifling (to) me. When I returned by half past six I heard already outside that our dear gentleman had been sent for by the Queen. My heart felt so full that big tears stole down my face and made me feel better. A lovely sunshine brightened his journey. God grant that all may turn out well. The moon rose silvery as he returned amongst loud cheers at night. Will he satisfy the people? Let us hope so. May the Almighty guide him to rule in love and truth.[4]

In 1883 Schlüter went with William and Catherine, Herbert and Mary on the voyage of the Pembroke Castle to Copenhagen. Zadoc, the valet, also went but Schlüter was in the more favourable position, and enjoyed being pampered when the sea was rough at the beginning of the voyage. 'I am just picking a chicken bone and a glass of champagne. They say it will be good for me,' she noted in her diary. She found a companion in Miss Fisher, Laura Tennant's maid, and together they enjoyed a novel:-

I am getting my sea legs on. I am knitting and Miss Fisher reads out to Which loved him best? One of those sensational novels, but very fair for the voyage.

In the evenings they were joined by the ship's doctor and chief engineer, 'and laughed and flirted until 10 p.m., then tumbled into our beds,' or played hide and seek on the big ship.

As was usual Schlüter was known to the family by her surname, although Mary and Helen's name for her was simply Schlüt. She lived close to the family, and yet not as one of them. She had her own suite of bedroom and sitting-room; and she was served by a cleaning maid, a cook to bring meals to her room, and a page on call to run errands. She made friends with Hyem, the butler, and his wife, and they with Mrs. Jolly, the head cook, formed the élite of the household hierarchy.

As the years went by the duties that Schlüter had originally been appointed for had all but evaporated. By 1885 Herbert was thirty and had been M.P.for Leeds for five years. Harry was in business in India. Helen was ensconced in Cambridge as Vice-Principal of Newnham College. The three elder ones of the family, Willy, Agnes and Stephy, were all married and had homes of their own. Then came the final catastrophe: Mary became engaged to be married to Harry Drew. The news was totally unexpected and came to Schlüter as a great shock, for it threatened her position and the life style she so much enjoyed. Mary, the last to live with her parents and Schlüter's undoubted favourite, was to be taken over by a husband.

Catherine used her ingenuity, realising Schlüter could not bear to leave the family; she was thirty-four and had been with them for seventeen years, and her own sisters had settled in America. Catherine already had her own ladies maid, Stume, also German. She did not want two maids. What she suggested was that Stume should go to the less strenuous position to work for Agnes at Wellington College. Agnes had a painful arthritic hip, and needed help.

Thus Schlüter came to be Catherine's personal maid, and remained happily with the family for some more years. She records Mr. Gladstone's kindness when he insisted on sitting on top of the carriage when he was quite elderly and it was raining, so that she could sit inside. Catherine took her to see her husband and two sons in parliament. They watched in the ladies' gallery behind the diagonal wire mesh. This enabled them discreetly to see the men sitting below, without being in sight themselves.

I went to the House of Commons, thanks to Mrs. Gladstone's kindness. How very interesting it is to hear the speeches and to see the gentlemen bob up and down.

On June 27th 1887, Schlüter recorded her birthday:-

. . . . my three faithful servants had arranged my room lovely, and I was startled when I got down to breakfast — but stop, I was woke up through lovely little voices singing at my bedroom door, the children from the Home. I thanked them and kissed them, and asked God to make me worthy of all the kindness shown to me. Then I went downstairs, where I found a lovely display of roses and a beautiful watch from Mr. and Mrs. Drew.

As Mary commented when eventually she saw the diary: 'the way she gives us all back seats while she occupies the front seat!'

In 1890 Auguste Schlüter returned to Hanover to take care of her elderly mother, but she still came back to Hawarden for occasional holidays. She died in 1917, and after the war had ended between the countries of her origin and her adoption Mary received her final letter:-

I trust this letter will find you when I am gone. I want you to know once more how you have cheered and brightened my life, and once more I want to thank you. There is nothing I can leave you, but if anyone has loved you, it was
    Your humble, Schlüt.

16
Zadoc

Why did Zadoc, Mr. Gladstone's faithful valet, disappear, and why did the family try to hush up the news, which soon got into the national press? On 13th December 1893, Lord Rosebery wrote to Catherine:-

Dear Mrs. Gladstone,
   I am sorry that in a fit of temporary insanity caused probably by the nervous system Zadoc has made an end of himself.
      Yours sincerely,
         JR[1]

What was the explanation of the brief note? Had Zadoc really made an end of himself in a fit of temporary insanity, and if so why?

Zadoc Outrem came from a large Liverpool family. There were six sons and two daughters. To relieve the mother of some of her children, it was arranged that the two daughters would be brought up at Catherine's orphanage at Hawarden. For a family that was desperately poor the plan of boarding out some of the children was common in Victorian times. The children had no father: he had either died or left home. It was very hard for Mrs. Outrem to find enough to feed the family, and she knew the girls would be well brought up and that, not being far from Liverpool, she would be able to see them. Therefore Sarah and Elizabeth lived at Broadlane orphanage, originally set up for destitute children from the cotton famine in Lancashire and for orphans whose parents had perished in London's cholera epidemic. When they were about fourteen Sarah and Elizabeth were found positions in domestic service, for which they would have considered themselves fortunate.

In 1870 at the age of sixteen their brother, Zadoc, was employed as a footman by Catherine. He was the same age as Herbert, and as time went by the whole family came to know him very well. After eleven years Zadoc was promoted when William's valet, Hyem, was married in June 1881, and he became butler, Zadoc took over his work as valet. The job was principally dealing with clothes, making sure his busy master had the right clothes for the right occasions, cleaning and doing repairs, folding, putting away and hanging up, drying out and cleaning shoes and hats, and packing and unpacking. When William and Catherine went to stay at grand houses they took the valet and ladies maid. It was usual to call senior members of staff by their surnames, but the family continued to address Zadoc in the way they had grown used to. As well as working as valet, he continued as footman, and would serve dinners at Downing Street. He also answered the doorbell and thus became familiar with guests, who recognised him and greeted him when they called.

During those eventful and busy years of the eighteen-eighties Zadoc and Schlüter often travelled with William and Catherine. Zadoc was not, of course, as well educated as Schlüter, nor in a position of such prestige in the household, but they got on well together, Schlüter taking the leading part. Although they were envied by the rest of the household, travelling was often uncomfortable as we know from their journey to the south of France in 1883. Catherine was just recovering from shingles and Mary and Stephy came too. Schlüter shared a compartment with Stephy — she referred to him as the Rector — and with Zadoc.

> When night came we lay ourselves down as best we could. Mr. and Mrs. and Miss Mary had a sleeping car, the Rector and I on a seat each, Zadoc on the floor.[2]

In 1887 William and Catherine went to Naples where they stayed for about two months in the summer. They took Mary — her husband Harry Drew was left behind — and Herbert with them: also Schlüter and Zadoc. Travelling with them was Mr. Stuart Rendel, Liberal M.P. for Montgomery and now the attendant satellite, with his two daughters, Maud and Daphne. Two years later Maud was to marry Harry. However, on this holiday it was Zadoc who formed an attachment — to Maud and Daphne's maid, Annie. Zadoc decided he would like to see more of Annie back in London, and although their jobs were very tying there was usually a spare hour or two when they could meet.

Five years later they became engaged, but it seems that Annie still had her doubts. The uncertainty made Zadoc anxious. At the same time it was noticed by the family that he had become less reliable. The cause was plain for all to observe, and it soon became evident to William and Catherine that he had a drinking problem. This was a dreadful worry. It was quite unsuitable for him to travel with his master, now very elderly, to important people's houses. There is no record that he stole, but he soon parted with his wages. William and Catherine hoped that by talking openly to him and being very firm the problem might be solved, but it gradually became worse. They knew that if they dismissed Zadoc he would not be able to find another position, and yet they felt they could not keep him. He had known the family since childhood; in effect he had become a member of the family and was intensely loyal. They were both extremely worried and often discussed what they could do.

It occurred to them to consult Sir Andrew Clark who would keep the matter confidential, and whose opinion they could count on. They felt it would be a relief to have his judgement and they looked forward to hearing his decision. The elderly doctor examined and questioned Zadoc. Zadoc must go, he announced.

It was, of course, out of the question. An alternative was that he could go for treatment to the Keeley Institute near Cromwell Road. This was to be his last chance. Catherine realised that if she wrote she might influence him more than speaking to him, which had been tried so often before:-

Oct. 18, 1893.

Zadoc,

I must write a few lines to say that we thank God that you agree to the proposal made. It has taken off a great weight from Mr. Gladstone for you may believe how much trial we have gone through on your account.

Believe me we shall do all we can to keep everything quiet and thus to help you in the trial and strengthen you. We require a few more days to further the arrangements, and whilst we wish you to come here we consider it best for all parties that you should only be here a few hours. You will be allowed to go to Downing Street for a few nights which will give time for making for you the best arrangements we can. Therefore to settle all this, you will delay a few days before leaving Liverpool.

May you continue strong in the resolution you have taken. It was your only chance. God grant that in the end all may be blessed; that you will have reason to thank God that before it was too late the Hand has been stretched out to you.

    I remain,
      your friend
        Catherine Gladstone

After three weeks at the Keeley Institute Zadoc was discharged with a report from the Secretary that seemed optimistic. After making a decision never to touch alcohol again Zadoc was to go on a prolonged holiday, visiting his married sisters in Liverpool, his friends at Holker Hall, Carnforth, other friends on the Isle of Man, and then to stay in Nottingham. He was soon short of money for both the married sisters in Liverpool persuaded him to give them some of his funds; no doubt their families were very poor, and Zadoc obliged in parting with a few pounds.

After a month away from London he returned to his work in Downing Street. A week later he told Wright, the butler, that he was going out for half an hour. He had arranged to meet Annie at the Duke of York steps, a convenient place between Downing Street and Mr. Rendel's home, to 'settle whether they would go on keeping company.' He did not return. Annie never saw him; she waited in vain. The next morning Wright reported to Herbert that Zadoc had been out all night. Herbert immediately sent a message to Harry: 'Will you come over as soon as you can for as yet I don't know what to make of it.' The responsibilities of the missing valet fell on Herbert and Harry. Their father was now nearly eighty and serving his fourth administration as Prime Minister: he was preoccupied with unemployment which each winter became increasingly serious. It was now December and delegations of unemployed men frequently called at Downing Street. One group hoped that the government would take over the building of new southern electric railway to create more jobs.

Herbert immediately contacted the police. Inspector William Conquest of Scotland Yard was put in charge of the investigation, and set about assiduously tracing and questioning Zadoc's relations and friends. The sisters in Liverpool declined to say how much money he had given them, and nobody knew where he had gone. Herbert's worst fears rose when Inspector Conquest wrote, 'these fresh facts strengthen the theory of suicide.' There were still no clues to why he had vanished, but the story was carried in a Sunday newspaper for all to read:-

Disappearance of Mr. Gladstone's valet
The Premier greatly distressed

The Central News says: 'We are in a position to confirm the rumours as to the mysterious disappearance of Mr. Gladstone's faithful valet. He has been missing for nearly a week, and it is gravely feared that some evil has befallen him. The Premier is greatly distressed.

The missing man is Mr. Zadoc Outrem, who for twenty-three years past has been the trusted friend, valet, and groom of the chamber to Mr. Gladstone. The Premier recently gave his valet a holiday. Outrem went to Liverpool and afterwards to Douglas, Isle of Man, whence he returned on the 22nd ultimo. He accompanied Mr. Gladstone on his recent visit to Windsor, and also to Brighton. He returned with his master to Downing Street, and remained there till Thursday week.

. . . . When he left Downing Street, Outrem was wearing a blue serge jacket with diagonal cloth waistcoat, dark striped tweed trousers, dark socks, laced shoes, dark overcoat and hard felt hat. He is described as 6 ft. in height, light brown hair, grey eyes, clean shaven lips, with very slight whiskers, and face somewhat blotchy. He was accustomed to smoke a pipe, carried his head on one side, was of rather slovenly gait, very reserved in manner and blunt in speech.[3]

Since Zadoc's disappearance the whole family and household were greatly concerned over what had become of him. They prayed for his return. On the other hand they had to consider how to treat him if he reappeared, which he might do at any time. Herbert and Harry tried to stay in at Downing Street as often as possible whilst their father was in the House of Commons. The old man was aggravated with the notion that Zadoc had been kidnapped or was being held hostage on his behalf. In a note from the House of Commons he wrote: 'The lack of news makes Outrem's absence more and more formidable. I am fearful he should have been got hold of by disrespectful people in the park.' At the same time he left a letter for Zadoc, should he return, with a strict warning that he might lose 'his title.'

If Zadoc did suddenly enter the house dealing with him would not be easy. Herbert and Harry knew that if their mother was in she would treat the wayward servant like a prodigal son, delighted to welcome him and install him in his former position. The consequences of such things happening, of her affection and forgiveness, they could scarcely bear to think about, as they consulted each other. It was never to happen. The sad facts came to light. Zadoc had been found near the Tower of London drowned in the Thames.

It was the 12th December that Inspector Conquest called at Downing Street to say Zadoc's body had been found. It had been identified by Police Constable Francis Outrem, his brother, who lived at Woolwich. It was ten days since the disappearance, ten days of agony for the family. Although their parents offered to go to the inquest, Herbert and Harry chose to represent them.

The inquiry relative to the death of Mr. Gladstone's valet, Zadoc Outrem, who mysteriously disappeared from the Premier's residence in Downing Street about a fortnight ago, and whose body was recovered from the Thames on Tuesday last, took place on Thursday in the library of the Tower, before Mr. Wynne Baxter. Mr. Herbert Gladstone, M.P., and Mr. Henry Gladstone were present throughout the proceedings . . . .

James Borer, waterman, deposed that on Tuesday morning at 11 he was proceeding in his boat near the Tower, and found the body between two ships. It was buried in 2 ft. of mud.

Coroner — How could you see it? I felt it with my staff. I was searching for things under the water, as I gain my living that way.

Witness, continuing, said that the body was fully clothed, with the exception of a hat. He attached a rope to it, and it was conveyed to the Tower Mortuary. He thought it had been carried for some distance by the tide to the spot where it was discovered. . . .

Mr. Wright, butler to Mr. Gladstone, said he saw deceased on the evening of 30th at Downing Street, when he asked the witness's permission to go out, stating that he had arranged to meet his young lady at the Duke of York's steps at half past eight. He went out and did not return, and on the following day the matter was placed in the hands of the police.

Coroner: Did he confide any love-affair to you? No. . . .

Mr. Herbert Gladstone said the deceased had been in the employ of the family for twenty-three years, and was a reliable, punctual, loyal and intelligent servant. The deceased was not a strong man, and had been under the treatment of influenza by Sir Andrew Clark, since when he had very bad health. The Jury returned a verdict that the deceased was found drowned, but how he got into the water there was no evidence to show.[4]

The funeral took place at Hawarden. Nearly every house and shop had its blinds drawn. The coffin of oak had massive brass fittings. Mrs. Outrem was present with her five sons, Joseph, Francis, John, Alexander and Ebenezer, and her two daughters, Sarah and Elizabeth. Catherine, Mary and Herbert attended the simple ceremony.

It was a drizzling December day. Amongst the flowers, a cross of arum lilies had been sent by William and Catherine and a wreath from the servants of Downing Street, nor was Zadoc forgotten by the girl he loved, for:-

A fine collection of everlasting flowers, arranged under a glass in a case was sent with a card bearing the following: 'In affectionate and loving remembrance of my dear friend' from Miss Hill, employed at Mr. Stuart Rendel's of London.[5]

17
John Ruskin

Of the many famous people the Gladstones came to know none generated more excitement than John Ruskin, the most renowned critic and lecturer of mid-Victorian Britain. At the time of his first visit in January 1878 he was fifty-eight, but appeared an old man. Such was his authority that the chance to meet, question, and even cast eyes upon him was looked upon as the opportunity of a life-time for the family.

John Ruskin, who had made his home at Brantwood, overlooking Lake Coniston, met Mary when she was staying nearby with her friend, Frances Graham, daughter of William Graham, a wealthy Liberal M.P. for Glasgow. In due course Mary asked her parents if she might invite him to stay at Hawarden, and a date was arranged for 11th January. He had suffered increasingly for several years from poor health and depression, and so it was hardly surprising that he wrote to Agnes saying he had changed his mind and would prefer not to come. She evidently knew him and he, no doubt, felt her to be sympathetic and willing to accept the excuse. But her husband, Edward Wickham, had already decided upon questions he would like to ask the great man, as had Willy and Stephy. In fact the whole family were greatly looking forward to the visit. Mary thought she might still persuade him to come so, as time was short, she sent him a telegram. He replied with a charming letter of apology, 'begging your merciful pardon,' saying he would come after all. The family still doubted whether he would come, having prepared themselves to be disappointed.

John Ruskin started from Brantwood in a carriage and drove over the hills to

catch the train at Windermere. He already had misgivings but felt too indecisive to turn back, and as the train drew into Chester his mind was full of new anxious thoughts. He did not think he was going to like his host, or his host's family, or their household. He was met at the station by a carriage which was also to pick up another guest, Henry Scott Holland, Canon of Christ Church, Oxford, who was looking forward to an easy, relaxing few days. John Ruskin did not realise that Canon Scott Holland knew the family well, and as the carriage jogged towards the house, the first-time visitor confided his forebodings that he had 'the darkest view possible of his host,' and that he was very likely to be called home by a telegram.

The young don was intrigued and waited for developments. He more than likely shared his secret with the younger members of the family, and he noticed the first evening John Ruskin mentioned he might be recalled by telegram several times, on Saturday a couple of times, and on Sunday not at all. How the family responded to his threats can well be imagined.

When he entered the drawing room and the heart of the family, Mary records, 'we were all unspeakably shy.' Such was his extraordinary presence that he readily held forth with opinions on the problems of the world, and everybody wanted to ask him his view on just about everything. He had a charming manner which they found most touching. Agnes's little girl, Katie, sensed this and was soon to be seen leaning up against his knee. Agnes then asked Katie to give him a bunch of violets, and as it was January violets would have been special. The violets were handed over, but when she was thanked Katie broke out with the truth: the violets were really Mama's.

The first evening Mary played the piano and Mr. Ruskin came over to talk to her and to Alfred Lyttelton, who was also staying.

> After dinner, Alfred and I got all the plums, as he sat by the piano with us. Ruskin spoke just as he writes. Every word might be profitably written down . . . . but heaps of what he says is purely visionary and impractical, and it is the ideal beauty of it which is so entrancing. . . . . he almost made one believe the ideal might became the real. Went off to bed in a glow.

The next day the conversations continued. Canon Scott Holland felt it necessary to get a winter game of lawn tennis going to relieve the tension; the elderly sage in frock coat and patent leather slippers remaining indoors because of his delicate health. News of the visit spread quickly. Lord Acton, invariably in touch with the family, turned up. To join the already large house party more appeared for dinner. The pure excitement generated by the visitor was unique. On Sunday the curate, Mr. Otterly, could hardly preach his sermon, he felt so shy of speaking before Mr. Ruskin.

On Monday the visit came to an end and life returned to normal. William noted in his diary how pleasant his guest had been:-

> Mr. Ruskin came; we had much conversation, interesting of course, as it must always be with him.

As soon as he got home John Ruskin wrote to his printer ordering him to cancel the page of his book which contained insults on Mr. Gladstone, and then wrote a letter of apology to Mary:-

> . . . . I have been grievously deceived concerning him myself, and have once written words about him which I trust you at least may never see. They shall be effaced henceforward; (I have written to cancel the page on which they are.) If ever you see them forgive me, and you will know what it is to forgive.
>
> And you will like having me with you again, then, in the autumn? I never can understand that people like me at all, if I like them. I'll read your letter over and over again, meantime; and am, indeed, myself to your Father and to you all,
>   Your grateful and loving,
>   John Ruskin.[1]

In the summer there were meetings in London and in October he was back for another visit to Hawarden; he remained a fond friend of the family for the rest of his life. In *The Stones of Venice*, a detailed and beautifully written work in three volumes still admired for its style, he revealed Venice as the merging of west and east, Christian and Moslem, Gothic and Byzantine. By analysing the buildings he exposed the character and emotions of the people who had created the city, and tempted an increasing number of British travellers to visit it. In the autumn of 1879 William, Catherine, Mary and Herbert went to Venice via Germany. The family had endured a tough couple of years on the political scene, and before setting off Mary commented that 'Papa looked rigid and Mama hot and excited,' and there was 'every sort of bother over our luggage.' However Herbert, now a don at Keble College, Oxford, was always cheerful.

In the middle of September they travelled on an overnight ship from Sheerness to Flushing, and caught the train to Cologne, where they stopped to see William's sister, Helen, pathetically ill and confused, who was to die the next year. Then on by train to Munich, and a carriage drive to Villa Arco on Tegernsee to stay with Lord Acton's family.

After a restful fortnight they set off for Venice, stopping two days in Innsbruck on the way. To cross the Dolomites into Italy they then rented a horse and cart, but it was scarcely large enough for the driver and four people and their luggage. Its redeeming feature was that it had springs, and the day was fine and the views of the mountain peaks were glorious. The four walked up the hill and then mounted the cart to go down hill. When they reached the frontier they paused for a picnic lunch under a tree. It may have been adequate but was hardly comfortable; there were ants on the ground and it began to drizzle. William, Mary and Herbert then walked another seven miles while Catherine rode in the cart. They then needed to change the horses, but none were available, the only alternative being to continue in a tiny carriage. Against their parents' wishes Mary and Herbert insisted on walking. Mary noted:-

> . . . . so we started, but their will was too strong for us and in spite of the danger and warnings we gave them, the older birds insisted on our getting on. For about half a mile we proceeded safely and then, crash seemed to go everything, and over each other we tumbled and rolled in the dust. It all felt so safe I could have no inclination but laughter not unmingled with triumph, and the parents' voices of intense tragedy inquiring how much they were hurt only added somehow to the comedy. Mama came down pretty sharply on her nose, but luckily no stones, and the road was good and safe and we were close to a house.

Herbert, who stayed put, could hardly believe his eyes as mother, sister, and father landed on top of each other. It was typical of the parents to be so concerned for each other that they forgot their own discomforts, so that when they fell out of the carriage it took a moment to reflect what had happened to their own bodies in the way of cuts and bruises. Fortunately help was close and the wooden axle of the little carriage was spliced and repaired for the remainder of the way to Venice. They also hired another rickety-looking carriage in which the older birds and Mary went, whilst Herbert continued in the tiny carriage with the luggage. Their spirits were not daunted because the magnificent scenery was a compensation for their discomforts.

On arriving in Venice Mary found a letter from Edward Burne-Jones, the artist, who knew the family well. He had lent her useful books to read, and now warned her the first view of the city might come as an anti-climax:-

> I wonder how you have looked at Venice, and whether, like all the greatest things in the world, it is a painful surprise at first, almost disappointment. It is the second-rate things that win at first, I think, and the greatest is always a little painful.

Soon another letter of advice arrived:-

> Don't be carried about to see things; Venice is the chief picture there, and don't weary your eyes with others, but get men to row you in and out of ALL the byways and watch every corner you turn. Windows and arches and gateways of the utmost beauty are ready to greet you at every turn, and don't go into churches and see pictures this time.

The holiday in Venice was utterly delightful and the family met several people they already knew, as well as having introductions from Mr. Ruskin and Mr. Burne-Jones. There seemed to be so many British people there that they were amused to discover that some were busy trying to avoid each other. The pleasures the family experienced gave them fresh strength, though little did they imagine what the tumultuous years of the eighteen-eighties would bring.

From his first visit to Hawarden, John Ruskin remained a loyal friend of the family. His favourite was Mary; for many years they corresponded at regular intervals. The admiration was mutual, but John Ruskin enjoyed revealing affection, writing to 'My dear little madonna,' or 'Darling Cecilia,' and once addressing the envelope to Sainta Cecilia (on account of her musicality) which the postman duly delivered. In them he would often send 'love to papa and mama,' and would sign off in a mode of adoration such as:-

> Please imagine me, bowing or kneeling as low as you please, and every gratefully and affectionately yours, J. Ruskin.

In these letters they shared private opinions and happily described the trivialities of life. John Ruskin also adored Agnes and Helen, who persuaded him to speak at Newnham College, Cambridge; but true to form they were not so forthcoming as the middle sister. Some of the letters to Mary and Helen were privately printed in 1903 under the title *Letters to M.G. and H.G. by John Ruskin*, and letters received by Mary of special interest have been published in the definitive edition of his works in 39 volumes, edited by Cook and Wedderburn, 1903-12.

18

The Election of 1880

The family met for Christmas 1879, as usual, at Hawarden, and as Mary was the one who had been with her parents on the Midlothian campaign she became the centre of attention. Since they had returned Mama had spent much time in her room recovering from exhaustion, whilst Papa, now sixty-nine, had returned 'as fresh as paint.' The three had travelled to Edinburgh in a saloon carriage, and come back using the same carriage which was just as well as they had returned with an assortment of presents for Papa: clothes, shirts, suits, tweed, a hat, gloves, rugs, plaids; not to mention many small items such as pencils. Catherine had also some unexpected gifts showered on her, whilst Mary had had flowers from the Women's Liberal Federation in Edinburgh, where the former 'still stately and beautiful' had spoken.

They had reached Edinburgh on a dark and frosty evening: the station was decorated in red, and a roar went up from the crowds kept back by barriers. Lord Rosebery met them and they mounted his open carriage drawn by four magnificent horses, surrounded by postilions. All along the road to Dalmeny House at South Queensferry, people were waiting, setting up a cry as the carriage came into view, and as they entered the park rockets and fireworks were set off.

Lord Rosebery was exceedingly rich: as well as inheriting Dalmeny and a London house, he spent much time at his house at Epsom, the Durdans, so that he could be near his racehorses. He had married Hannah Rothschild, who had inherited Mentmore and a fortune to go with it. Lord Rosebery, a future Prime Minister, had begun to make his mark in politics but he was first and foremost a racing man and as such enjoyed a thrill to the finish. It was he who made the arrangements for Mr. Gladstone to contest the constituency of Midlothian, hoping to oust the Earl of Dalkeith from his Conservative seat. Midlothian consisted of Edinburgh and the area surrounding it. The campaign started in November 1879, though parliament was not dissolved until March 1880.

Naturally the family wanted to hear the details as Mary described the many political meetings and the luxurious life at Dalmeny. She also told of the pinched, haggard, eager faces of the men who had surrounded and caught hold of the carriage when they went to meetings. The greatest crowd had gathered at the Waverley Market, then an enclosed and covered area, where it was said 18,000 were standing. The press had protected themselves from the crush

as their tables and chairs were enclosed by a barricade, which looked like a curious kind of cage. The speeches from the high platform were constantly interrupted by repetitive shouts, but as they went on and on there were screams of 'help' and 'water;' and when people fainted the limp bodies were transported over the heads of the packed crowd to the only space where they could be laid down, the journalists' table. Those on the platform became absorbed by the expressions of disgust, as the press attempted to note down the speech with bodies lying in front of them.

In the evening the house party would relax at Dalmeny House, built in the best Victorian gothic style overlooking the long lawns to the Firth of Forth. After dinner five pipers appeared to play and march three times round the table. The Marquis of Aberdeen and his wife, Ishbel, were staying, and sometimes Lord Rosebery would coax him to demonstrate his party game of making various train whistles. As a boy he had observed the different whistle used by signalmen and could brilliantly imitate them. But to demonstrate his skills he needed someone to sound like a train. William would then do the chuff-chuffing which would be controlled by the various whistle signals much to the amusement of the assembled guests. The campaign of a week ended with a magnificent torchlight procession through the streets of Edinburgh. Lord Rosebery had brought the idea back from America, which proved very popular.

The second week was spent travelling. The national papers were full of the Midlothian campaign for it was an election on a new scale. Never before had a parliamentary leader planned moving from place to place with speeches to anticipated audiences with such precision, and, incidentally, making use of the railway to do so, regarded as most ungentlemanly by his opponents. The result was that the Liberal message had reached 86,000 in a fortnight.

When the date of the election was announced in March, Willy set off to stay with the Lytteltons at Hagley Hall, as he had been selected as Liberal candidate for East Worcestershire. The Lyttelton cousins, and indeed their father, had recently become backers of the Liberal cause, and Charles, the eldest, had thought of standing himself but was a nervous speaker. To them Willy seemed self-assured; as Neville commented, 'he was a quiet, unassuming man with none of the fiery zeal of his father, but quite an effective platform speaker.' In contrast to the immense enthusiasm generated by his father's unrivalled skill as a popular orator and the pent-up energy which he unleashed on his vast audiences, Willy's campaign in Worcestershire was mild and unexciting.

For the election of 1880 the private ballot was used, as it had been in 1874, following the Bill passed in 1872. Previous to that voters had mounted a platform to state their vote to a clerk, and every hour or so during the day the poll was made known. One might have thought that the private ballot would improve behaviour at elections; in fact the opposite was true. The elections of 1874 when the Conservatives won decisively and 1880 when the Liberals were swept in with a huge majority, were noisy, boisterous, and deceitful. When Willy arrived at Stourbridge a man was selling pamphlets stating that his father had committed suicide. The man was later arrested, but at the same time another speaker was quoting an epitaph in verse.

The constituency to the south of Birmingham, included the market towns of Stourbridge, Selly Oak, Bromsgrove and Droitwich, and was mainly agricultural. Probably the two Conservatives thought they would safely retain their seats, for Sir R. Temple did not arrive from Bombay till a few days before the ballot. The other, Mr. Allsopp, the owner of a local brewery was much 'prevented from active duty by an attack of his old enemy, the gout.'[1]

The two Liberal candidates were Willy and Mr. G. W. Hastings who lived at Malvern. They announced they were sound agricultural reformers and would restrict food imports which had reached £100 Mn. a year. Asked about flogging in the army Willy said every other country in Europe had abolished it and he would be sorry if the British Army was the only one to retain it. The main issue was whether the British troops should be withdrawn from South Africa and Afghanistan, and at Bromsgrove, where the Liberals concentrated their meetings trying to win over the Conservatives, he said:-

> With regard to the issues at present before the country he thought there were signs everywhere that the dream of Jingoism and Imperialism which had so long divided the land was being dispelled, and that the people were determined to once more place their confidence in the Liberal cause.

The close result of the poll was declared opposite the workhouse at Droitwich. Each person on the electoral register had two votes:-

| W. H. Gladstone (L) | 4,879. | Sir R. Temple (C) | 4,417. |
| G. W. Hastings (L) | 4,833. | H. Allsopp (C) | 4,258. |

With the election imminent Herbert had left his position as Keble College, Oxford, to become his father's secretary. Unprepared, he was pressed to become a candidate himself. Willy was equally surprised. He wrote:-

> How plucky of you to go in for that fearful piece of work in Middlesex. I was perfectly amazed this morning to hear it. God speed you. I am sick of this already, though it has only just begun, but I think our chance good.

Indeed, the constituency of Middlesex proved to be 'a fearful piece of work,' as Herbert soon learnt. Mary always accompanied him, and noted as they went to a meeting in Kilburn, 'great hall, great noise.' Then in a Brougham 'we flew though quiet country lanes and budding hedges to Harlesden,' where they were rapturously received, but the next day:-

> On to Finchley, where it was horrid, great row and series of fights, pepper and snuff freely scattered. We all coughed and sneezed. Herbert spoke vigorously to the reporters.

Hallam Tennyson, who was with them, discovered afterwards that his watch had been stolen, but driving themselves home in a tub in the moonlight revived their spirits. The next meeting at Tottenham had a strong group of Imperialists who prevented Herbert being heard by roaring 'Rule Britannia,' so they left for Enfield which was equally rowdy, but Herbert held their interest by speaking on foreign policy. As they left for the station, to their surprise, they found themselves being cheered:-

> Coming out we found the horses had been taken from the carriage, and with runners harnessed and torches flaring and cheers ringing we flew down to the station, where Herbert was seized by a frantic mob and carried on their shoulders. After an ardent farewell got home about 12.

There were other noisy meetings at Southgate, Mill Hill, and Hendon; then all rural villages. Herbert spurred himself on, but the result on April 5th was devastating, with Herbert coming bottom of the poll. However, Mr. W. E. Forster, the Liberal cabinet minister who had promoted the Elementary Education Act, had watched Herbert speak at Kilburn when the chair he was standing on gave way, and Mr. Forster thought he had managed very well. Impressed with the incident of the broken chair which hardly seemed fortuitous, he introduced Herbert to join the City Liberal Club and asked him to speak. Mr. Forster was member for Bradford, a safe Liberal seat. He recommended Herbert for Leeds, a constituency that had hoped to have his father as their representative. At a meeting of the Liberal Four Hundred of Leeds, Herbert was formally approved, and an outside meeting in the Coloured Cloth Hall Yard was planned to hear him speak.

Catherine accompanied her youngest son. He was twenty-six but with pink rounded cheeks and thick springy hair he looked younger. The size of crowds is always open to dispute, but if the *Leeds Mercury* report is reliable this must have been one of the biggest political meetings ever held. A very high wooden platform had been erected in front of the Coloured Cloth Hall, and the yard was known to hold between thirty-three and thirty-four thousand people. Two hours before the commencement of speeches it was filled, but:-

> It was only in appearance, for the fresh comers searched out all the spare places and nooks and spaces, and gradually worked deeper and deeper into the yard, until the mass was solidified and cemented into one compact and gigantic human body.

The mass of people, waiting in a high state of excitement, were excellently entertained by some climbing feats:-

> Some additional excitement and amusement was furnished by a number of venturesome persons who, determined to have a good view of the candidate and his illustrious mother, ascended by means of the water spouts running up the sides of the buildings to the roof, and then scrambled along until they reached the pinnacle and spread themselves along the slopes of the gables of the Hall. . . . . Great merriment was caused by the case of one individual, who having reached the

top of the spout found himself destitute of the strength necessary to raise himself onto the roof, but the friendly hands of more successful predecessors soon hoistered him up, amid the cheers, laughter and applause of the spectators.

First there was a procession of banners, then Mrs. Gladstone, leaning on the arm of the Chairman, Mr. J. Kitson, then Herbert led others to the platform. The noise was quietened by the use of a trumpet and then there was some little wait because someone had fainted, but as soon as the body was removed out of the crush Mr. Kitson spoke, saying any opposition to Herbert was a dreary joke: this was received in true Yorkshire style by grins and cheerful laughter. Herbert, who must have shouted to be heard at all, said it was the greatest occasion of his life, which of course was true. When he said, 'if I am elected,' there were outbursts of laughter proving that the audience looked upon the idea of opposition as a tremendous joke for, it seems, nobody present was a Conservative. The day stayed fine; he spoke for three quarters of an hour and, on finishing, was met with an outburst of cheering from thirty thousand pairs of lungs. There were then calls for Mrs. Gladstone to speak, and she came to the front of the platform and bowed. Mr. Kitson said her voice was not sufficiently strong; but Herbert had been born in Downing Street: further roars of laughter. It was true he had been born in 11, Downing Street, when his father was Chancellor of the Exchequer.

There were other meetings, including the Women's Liberal Federation. The Conservatives had recently started the Primrose League, realising how valuable women could be at the time of an election, and the Liberals had followed suit. Whilst Herbert had not been prepared for questions on women's suffrage, Catherine had sensibly got her husband to put into words her thoughts, so she said, on a piece of paper she carried around. In short she said that it would come, but there were other more urgent needs, such as better education and health to come first.

The declaration of the poll took place in front of the Town Hall a week later, when Herbert and Catherine again appeared to find a vast crowd, mainly of men wearing bowler hats. This time two photographers stood on the platform taking photographs of the crowd. The sun was bright and warm and every window was filled with ladies who had dressed in their best hats for the occasion. When Mr. Kitson said, 'Will he do?' no opponent spoke; and Herbert was elected little knowing that he would remain as member for thirty years. As he and his mother left the carriage that took them to the station was cascaded with primroses as it drew along Boar Lane.

During the coming years much correspondence followed from the Mayor of Leeds, Mr. Joseph Henry, tall and striking with an untiring ardour for his city and their young member. 'I have a way of speaking out what I think,' he wrote; and 'what we have wanted in Leeds is leaders with more dash.' When thanked he revealed:-

You say truly that I do not care for gush but I am free to admit that your kind words and wishes are welcome.

The next year Mr. Gladstone visited Leeds. It was said by the family to be the greatest reception he had in his life. The Prime Minister was unfortunately suffering from lumbago, so he always appeared arm in arm with Mayor Henry, which looked rather well. In one hall where people had waited a long time on a summer's day to keep their place the lack of air became so serious that part of the roof was torn away to prevent people suffocating. In between meetings the party drove around in three tubs, and the factory girls who lined the routes wore brightly coloured shawls and yellow paper hats.

Various modes of transport could be seen in the London streets. The rich were recognised by their carriages. Lord Rosebery chose to drive his own carriage and pair, and Earl Spencer, known as the Red Earl for his hair and beard, liked to ride and to ride fast. He particularly enjoyed a brisk canter up St. James's Street and along Piccadilly on his way to Hyde Park. Bicycles were just coming in, and Arthur Balfour loved his bicycle, but William walked miles and miles in London. He thought nothing of setting off for Hampstead or Putney at a vigorous pace, but with the increasing traffic he did not like crossing arterial roads. Edward Hamilton, his Private Secretary, noted that though he never feared for his own safety as a politician, his anxiety was apparent when crossing crowded thoroughfares:-

> The only occasion on which his natural nervousness showed itself — and that was only during the last two decades of his life — was when he was crossing a crowded thoroughfare. He then behaved like a proverbially timid nursery-maid, who commences her transit with a run halfway across the street, suddenly stops short, and beats an equally hasty retreat. Owing to such nervous vacillation, partly attributable to the vast development of street traffic in his old age, he would have met with more frequent accidents during his walks in London, had it not been that cabmen and omnibus drivers, quick to recognise him would pull up to let him pass by; and to this consideration on their part he constantly alluded with gratitude.

19

10, Downing Street

The family moved into 10, Downing Street in early May 1880, wondering what the future would hold. Amidst the unpacking there was much bustle, and all the time people coming and going, and carriages kept arriving bringing flowers. Nobody had time or inclination to arrange them, and the beautiful spring flowers were placed in jugs and basins on the stone floor of the entrance hall. The family lived and slept on the first floor, the ground floor consisting of the big reception rooms, the dining room, the cabinet room and the offices where the secretaries worked.

Heating was by coal fires and lighting by gas and oil lamps. There were cupboards and shelves but no filing cabinets. In the stationery cupboard was much that is familiar today: headed paper, flimsy paper for copies, envelopes, paper clips, notebooks, telegram forms, tape for tying bundles of letters together and so forth. There were wooden tables and desks and wooden chairs, with the odd carpet on the floor. On the tables there would be blotters, ink pots, pens, pen cleaners, and pencils. There were no typewriters or adding machines.

Typewriters were not much used until the 1890's. William presented Willy with a typewriter in about 1887, but there were none in Downing Street. That is not to say typewritten letters were not occasionally received. Letters from General Booth, who had only recently formed the Salvation Army, came in large typewritten script, and Andrew Carnegie's letters from America were always typewritten. Occasionally typewritten letters would arrive in a fancy sloping script, but these were a rarity. All correspondence was handwritten, and many letters had to be copied.

The five secretaries who had been chosen through personal contact, felt it a great honour to work in 10, Downing Street. They seem to have been on friendly terms with each other, and were known to the family by their Christian names.

One secretary lived on the premises, usually the first secretary. Arthur Godley, the first secretary in 1880, and his wife enjoyed their flat on the top floor, which also helped with expenses. He was paid a modest salary: half from the government and half from the Prime Minister who, of course, received no salary and had few costs reimbursed. Arthur Godley had been a private secretary since 1872 and was much valued, but he found his increasing responsibilities a great strain. After two years back at Downing Street he resigned, and became a

Commissioner of the Inland Revenue, where he had a better salary and a secure job. Incidentally, his wife found one of her small duties a strain: that was taking a cup of tea and bread and butter for one into cabinet meetings, when weary eyes foretold her that all those round the table were ready for a similar little pick-me-up.[1]

Edward Hamilton then became first secretary to his surprise, as he was not the most senior of the secretaries. In every way he subsequently showed he deserved the promotion. Eddie was the only son of the Bishop of Salisbury, short in stature and a prodigious worker. He was nicknamed 'the cob.' Horace Seymour was brother of Lady Spencer, wife of the 'Red Earl' and known as the Fairy Queen; he was described as charming and hardworking in that order. He was replaced by Henry Primrose, also a great worker, and known as 'the Colonel,' as he had a fine moustache and looked the part. Sadly, all these men died young.

Herbert, now Member of Parliament for Leeds, also helped the secretaries now and then. Mary was made 'Honorary Private Secretary,' a new title for someone who did invaluable work and was always on call, but happened to be a woman. She worked in her own room on the first floor, and Helen would come home from Cambridge during vacations to help or to take over from her. Mary's special hidey-hole was the housemaids' cupboard, a little room for storing brooms, mops, etc., with enough space for a small table and a chair or two. With no window, it could be made into a cosy hole for one or two. Here privacy could be assured either to work at papers, have a quiet read, or share a secret.

Spencer Lyttelton, fourth of the Lyttelton brothers and sixth in the family, was the only secretary who had learnt to write shorthand, but he did not use this at No. 10. He found the endless correspondence tedious.

George Leveson-Gower was an assistant secretary and very much liked. Catherine would say of him, 'George is so intelligent, such luck!' A nephew of Lord Granville, he was given his post just down from Oxford University. The summer of 1880 was exceptionally hot, and George was feeling very tired because he had just finished his final exams; since when he had been going to dances which led to late nights. He settled down to his task of copying government communications on flimsy paper. First he decided to open the window wide of his pokey office overlooking the bit of garden at the back of No. 10. Then he was tempted to sit in his little arm-chair. To his intense embarrassment the boss entered, the papers took off and flew everywhere, but there was no reproval. George explained, 'I've just finished doing my exams,' to which the answer was, 'Oh, I daresay you are very tired.'

One night at the end of July the temperature never went below 90 degrees F. William and Catherine did not go to bed all night. The only way they could endure the heat was by constantly moving around.

First thing the post was sorted by the secretaries, then selected letters were taken up to the study after breakfast. William wrote many letters himself and always wrote the Queen 'a letter describing the proceedings of each sitting in the House of Commons, besides one after every cabinet meeting.'[2]

Each weekday, including Saturdays, when the post was opened letters were arranged into several baskets, according to the probable reply. Letters were first folded into an approximately uniform size: usually by folding the paper double, and then into three. This was, of course, the way letters were folded before envelopes were used. On the outside was written the date of arrival, name of sender, with a note on the content and answer required.

With the great increase in the quantity of correspondence it was decided to use a lithograph form for various replies. For example, to numerous letters the answer was 'no.' They went into a basket labelled 'Regret, Inability,' and could be answered with one lithograph form. To many people who thought they had landed on a good idea to write in the first place, to get a letter consisting of a single sentence, though a lengthy one, must have caused disappointment. What were these letters? They included 'begging letters, suggestions that Mr. Gladstone should advertise a patent food or medicine, deliver a lecture in support of a charity, give a post to the deserving nephew of the applicant (generally a lady) etc., etc.' The secretary would then reply using the lithograph form and write: 'Dear Sir,' or 'Dear Madam,' or 'Gentlemen,' and sign his own name at the bottom.

The secretaries also had to draw up lists for formal receptions. One particular evening was badly attended. The trays of clean glasses and uneaten food demonstrated that only half the people expected had come. Why so many dodged the invitation nobody could understand; and the family, the secretaries, and the domestic staff wondered if it was because of something they still did not know about. What was so puzzling was that the persons who had not attended could not be placed in any one category. How ungrateful of them not to come!

Then one of the secretaries made an observation. Nobody whose name began with a letter in the second half of the alphabet had attended. Soon the mystery was solved, for under a cushion on the drawing room sofa were hidden half the invitations, never sent out. Until the reception which turned out to be half a reception took place, the family had always written out the invitations themselves. From then on the job was given to the secretaries.

From time to time Mary and Helen attended drawing rooms, as the big receptions were known, at Buckingham Palace. Mary found making conversation easy, but Helen though more shy was not unoriginal: she once took in a bouquet of cowslips which she had picked near Cambridge. It was much admired. On the other hand Catherine once had pressed on her by Lady Hayter a bouquet of primroses to carry at a drawing room, just because she was not in the Primrose League, the stonghold of Conservative volunteers.

Both Mary and Helen found they were often called upon to do the flowers for dinner parties and receptions. When an important event was to take place the flower arrangements were a big item. The rooms and the halls were enormous. They realised that wild flowers are invariably the most beautiful, and perhaps the experience of having known John Ruskin urged them to use their own ideas. For a big Foreign Office reception Helen did the main room entirely with white daisies and various leaves, fern and grasses. After buying seven dozen glass vases, she and her friend, Lady Stephney, set to work. Catherine, Herbert, sister-in-law Annie, and Mrs. Jolly, the cook who had been with them years and years, exhorted their efforts. Helen wrote to Mary:-

> We did labour; she for about five hours, and I for about six hours. Mama, Annie, Mrs. Jolly, and Herbert especially joining in loud chorus of praise. Ivy, as you did last year, and about 110 different sized glasses of daises and feathery grass standing out of fern and delicate lily of the valley leaves and hawthorn tips. All the colour supplied by the uniforms.

Then she confided to Mary:-

> The F.O. party was a fine sight, the flowers beating all former F.O. parties into sticks.

Although various members of the family came and stayed occasionally they did not join in the grand dinners and receptions, which were often for men only. They frequently went off to spend time with the Lyttelton cousins. Mary also enjoyed doing table decorations with wild flowers. For a dinner party she used may and chestnut leaves. To Helen she was not modest about her efforts:-

> Masses of flowers came in; on hind legs all day arranging them. . . . . Two huge dinner parties. Came in to see the gents having their coffee, the two dinners amalgamated, and the evening was a success. I arranged one table, covering it with chestnut and may, quite lovely and all done in an hour. The Mentmore gardener took eight hours over the other and it was not half as pretty.

As well as loaning his chef, Lord Rosebery had sent his gardener. Very young-looking, excessively rich, and often about the house himself, he made the most outrageous remarks which made everybody smile. 'How is the great dictator, today?' he would ask, and then he would have a go at Catherine, 'Mrs. Gladstone, when are you going to let me have your photograph?' She loved it, but Mary chose to avoid him, for like some of the satellites he would ask her to put a request or idea to her father. Generally, the satellites, as Mr. Gladstone's unpaid admirers were known by others than the family, were invaluable, particularly at political meetings, when one or two were usually in evidence. They were apt to appear at No. 10 just in case they were needed.

When visitors with no appointment called it was the duty of one of the secretaries to see them and, if necessary, act as a buffer. George Leveson-Gower thought an Australian who appeared to ask how much a peerage would cost was mad, but then realised that he was being serious, and gave a 'frosty' reply.

George also tells the story, no doubt true, of Catherine talking to the Russian Ambassador at a Foreign Office reception. Catherine was by herself, and was asked where her husband was. Instead of saying he had stayed at home because he was recovering from 'flu, she replied to the astonished Russian Ambassador with one of her family expressions. George reported what he heard of the conversation:-

> 'Well,' she said with one of her confidential winks and nods, 'the fact is, he's rather dragging his leg.' (By this she meant he was a little tired.) The poor Ambassador, however, took it literally and cabled home in code that the Prime Minister had had a slight paralytic stroke.

Life was always under pressure at Downing Street with a secretary on duty on Sundays and even on Christmas Day. The one day in the year when work came to a halt was when the Queen took the review on Horse Guards Parade, for an excellent view may be obtained from the back of Downing Street. A stand was erected in the garden, and friends of the family were invited. The domestic staff were there. All the secretaries left their desks to mix with their own guests.

On November 8th 1882, it was a foggy, gloomy morning and impossible to see the trees in the park. The crowd could be heard but not seen, but Edward Hamilton noted in his diary that once again there had been the proverbial Queen's weather:-

> The review by Her Majesty on the Horse Guards Parade yesterday was a really beautiful spectacle and went off most successfully. There never could have been an occasion when the proverbial fortune of the Queen as to weather was demonstrated with such extraordinary exactness. The morning opened with a dense white fog. It lifted about eleven; but there was still a veil of mist which precluded a sight across the Parade till the arrival of the Queen, when instantly the curtain, as it were, rose and the spectacle was lit up by the appearance of the sun . . . .[3]

For the Gladstones there were occasional visits to Windsor Castle, and to stay in the same suite they had been in seven years before. Catherine spoke of the snug yellow rooms — snug perhaps compared to the state apartments — and the friendly faces of the staff, but more frequently there were visits, Saturday till Monday, to Sandringham. On a visit in November 1880, they were the only guests. They watched Princess Maud jumping her Arab horse in the afternoon. Then the Prince and Princess of Wales spoke of their concern at the appalling poverty of the Irish, and the injustices of tenant eviction which had led many to rebel and join the Land League. Having left the men to talk in the evening, Catherine was taken aback when Princess Alexandra called to say goodnight just as she was preparing for a night in a cold bedroom:-

> As I was in the act of pulling on last garments to go to bed a little tap on the door — soon peeped in Princess, so dear and amused. Looking all around to see our messiness, offering in fun to help me, and in the end tucking me up in bed.[4]

There was also conversation on how to cook a cheap dish. The Prince of Wales wrote to thank Catherine for the practical, if unusual book she sent after this stay:-

My dear Mrs. Gladstone,

Please accept my best thanks for you kind letter and for sending me the book 'How to cook the Yarmouth herring'!! which will be both useful and acceptable.

I can well understand how anxious and hard at work Mr. Gladstone must be over Ireland. The accounts I receive from letters and from those I have seen on coming over from there, are quite deplorable. What we hear and read of does not come up, I am told, to what is really taking place there. All the respectable farmers are being forced to join the Land League, and their sites and homes are in danger.

With the Princess's best regards,

    I remain,

        Yours very sincerely,

          Albert Edward.[5]

20

Security

Catherine did her best to try and persuade her husband not to walk home after dinner parties. Lady Jeune, a famous hostess, did her best to stop him having indigestion by serving plain puddings at her dinners much to others' disappointment, but she could not prevent William and Catherine walking home. They said that walking after an evening spent with friends made for refreshing sleep, which no doubt, it did.

One day in February 1881, Herbert was warned by the police that it was unsafe for his father to walk from the House of Commons to Downing Street, so he hired a growler. Growlers were four-wheeled cabs with wheels so old they growled as they turned: they had previously spent many years in private hands, and were therefore much the worse of wear. He wrote to Harry describing the situation: 'of course in all probability there is nothing to it.' This was the usual tone of the family: 'there is not the slightest cause for uneasiness.' Evidently there was enough unease in his mind to confide in Harry. Herbert wrote:-

> . . . . On the night of February 4th, the day you left, we had been dining with the Jeune's, and I walked back with Father to the House. I noticed we were followed by two policemen in plain clothes, who had followed Father from the House to the Jeune's. On passing through the lobby I was stopped by an Inspector of Police who showed me a telegram received from the Glasgow police to the effect that information had been received that Mr. Gladstone's life would be attempted that night! Of course in all probability there is nothing in it, but I saw Harvard Vincent and he was anxious that Father should not walk back from the House. So we trumped up a story of rough fellows being about who might annoy him, and I took him home in a four-wheeler. I was so amused because he grumbled as loud as the growler itself. Since then we manage that he should generally drive to and fro, and he varies the time he leaves the House as well as the door by which he goes out, so there is not the slightest cause for uneasiness.[1]

It was not only assassins that had threatened William's life. Three months after he had been made Prime Minister he caught typhoid, and the family had to stay in London until the end of August instead of going to the country, waiting till he was fit to travel. Dr. Andrew Clerk was always chosen as physician, for as well as being a friend and an interesting conversationalist, he managed to defend his patient. As soon as he had made the diagnosis the doctor started to send out bulletins of an improvement, though for some days the patient's condition was critical, as was realised by the Queen. Telegrams would arrive, brief and to the point, asking, 'How is Mr. Gladstone this morning,

VR,' and 'How is Mr. Gladstone this evening VR.' One wonders how Catherine replied to them.

The Queen suffered a terrifying experience when she was shot at when approaching Windsor station by a man called McLean. Later in court he was declared mentally deranged and sent to a criminal lunatic asylum for life, which in those days meant until he died a natural death. Her Majesty felt the punishment too lenient as she naturally felt anxious that the would-be assassin might escape, or that others would not be deterred. Despite the late hour she sent off a telegram to Downing Street, this time in cipher, although the opinion of the Prime Minister had nothing to do with the verdict. Edward Hamilton, the private secretary, had to get out of bed to deal with it. As he deciphered the telegram he must have been rather surprised as he came to the words 'half-cracked.'

> . . . . The moment she had received the result of the trial yesterday evening, she fired off to Mr. G. a long cipher telegram, which reached me after I had gone to bed. If half-cracked men of such dangerous propensities are to be acquitted on the ground of insanity, there will never be an end to them till they have wounded or killed her. One can't help sympathising with these very natural fears of a sovereign and woman combined . . . .[2]

From time to time bombs, referred to as dynamite explosions, were set off during the eighteen-eighties. In February, 1884, one went off in Victoria station and news of the blast made people wonder where the next might be detonated. The following January three bombs were planted by terrorists on a Saturday; one in the House of Commons, one in Westminster Hall, and one in the Tower of London, though fortunately no one was hurt.

When protection was necessary police closely followed William, but he was intolerant of his shadow, as he called his guard, and freely made his objection known. When a special detective with a revolver was appointed, the news was in the newspapers for all to read and be warned. The family took it all in their stride. The armed detective would follow on walks at a discreet distance, apparently not reacting to any of the conversation which went on as it always had done.

The detectives sometimes wore plain clothes or sometimes wore disguise. Lady Dorothy Neville describes a footman standing behind Mr. Gladstone's chair at a banquet, and another across the table standing facing him. Perhaps his guests wondered why it was necessary to have footmen who never handed round dishes. In any case Lady Dorothy Neville explains in her memoirs that everybody knew who the footmen were except the man they guarded who had no idea! Another common guise for the detective was to sit on the box of the carriage. This was where Willy found himself when the Marquis of Aberdeen, a skilled horseman, was called upon to drive the carriage in an emergency.

Better horses recently had been purchased by the Gladstones when Lord and Lady Aberdeen stayed at Hawarden at the beginning of December 1885, as a precaution against being held up whilst travelling. Willy, in particular, knew he would feel more at ease if his parents could have their carriage pulled by first-class horses that could move fast in the case of emergency. However, the new horses needed a skilled hand to drive them. An invitation was accepted by William, Catherine, and Helen, to dine and stay the night with Sir John Bankes, a local squire and family friend and, incidentally an arch Conservative, who lived at Soughton Hall, a drive of some four miles. The Marquis and Marchioness of Aberdeen were staying with the Gladstones, but were not going with them to Sir John Bankes. In their book, *We Twa*, they describe the frightening state of affairs:-

> . . . . the nights were very dark and the police had warned the P.M.'s secretaries that an attempt on Mr. Gladstone's life might be made, and that they (the police) had arranged without informing Mr. Gladstone that constables should be posted at intervals all along the road between the two houses.

All was in preparation. The threats would be overcome if the carriage drove fast and by an indirect route. Then, horrifically, the head coachman was taken ill and was unable to drive. The second coachman had injured his hand. Who would drive the carriage?

Nobody was willing to face the elderly Prime Minister and tell him that he was in danger and that an attempt might be made on his life, or deemed it sensible to warn him. In secrecy the police passed on their fears to the secretaries, who told the family, who even told their guests. Willy had reservations over driving the horses, which he felt he might have difficulty in controlling in the event of a confrontation. The Aberdeens heard the family discussing their dilemma, unwilling to withdraw from the invitation, but wondering whoever could drive the new horses. Recording the event in *We Twa*, Ishbel Aberdeen told her version of the story:-

> Hearing the discussion, A volunteered his services, and it was agreed Mr. and Mrs. Gladstone should not be let into the secret, for fear they might demur to A acting as coachman.

Schlüter, Catherine's maid, tells the story differently. According to her account Ishbel and Catherine connived behind their husbands' backs. Ishbel first consulted Catherine and then suggested to her husband that he should drive, which he readily accepted to do.

So it was arranged. Lord Aberdeen would drive and Willy would sit beside him as second coachman, directing him as to the route. They must have enjoyed dressing up for the part, and at the appointed hour the carriage was waiting in the dark at the front door. But before he and Catherine left, William wanted to say goodbye to the Aberdeens. Ishbel was there, but where was her husband? He, of course, could not be found in the house. Playfully, Ishbel helped in the search. The intrigue by now had really gone too far. As she left with her parents, Helen, who had kept her opinions to herself could bear it no longer, but Ishbel, tall and well-built compared to her slim, lithe husband, said she would pass on farewell messages to him.

William, Catherine, Helen, and Schlüter then got into the carriage. It was Schlüter who was so amused and knew that it would appeal to Lady Aberdeen's sense of humour, that she wrote her a letter describing the conversation in the carriage. Apparently Catherine mentioned that the carriage would be returning that night, and William asked why, because it was usual when they went to the Bankes for the carriage to remain at Soughton Hall. Catherine said:

'No dear, I thought it best for you to return tomorrow in the Victoria.'

To which he replied: 'How is that? A strange change of plans.' Helen could bear it no longer. Her father demanded to know why Zadoc the valet had not come with them.

'Oh Mamma, you'd better tell father the truth,' she said.

So then the truth came out. The Marquis was the coachman and Willy was sitting beside him, and Zadoc had been sent on ahead to open the gate to Soughton Hall to avoid delay. The occupants of the carriage all burst out with laughter. On reaching Soughton Hall the Marquis and Willy jumped off the box, took down the luggage and put it inside the front door, before driving off again into the dark night.

21

The Pembroke Castle

In July 1877 the Gladstones spent a pleasant few days on the Dublin Castle cruising along the south coast of England. Donald Currie had founded the Castle Line of sailing ships in 1862 going to Calcutta, and by 1872 he had steamers going to South Africa.

In 1880 William had been suffering from influenza, and Donald Currie, a Liberal M.P., had arranged another cruise on the Grandtully Castle, a bigger vessel of 3,600 tons displacement. It was felt, curiously, that this would assist his health, but he never was a person who liked the sea, nor was Catherine a good sailor. However, there was nothing like sea air for a return to vigour. Stephy, Helen, Harry, and Herbert accompanied their parents. Dr. Andrew Clark and Arthur Godley, the Principal Private Secretary, were also included, as was Sir James Lacaita, who could not stick the voyage and got off at Mull. They departed from Charing Cross station and were somewhat surprised to find it decked out in red cloth and fenced with barriers as if for royalty.

Boarding the Grandtully Castle at Gravesend, they steamed along the south coast to Dartmouth. On the way they happened to come across the Prince of Wales in his yacht who, on recognising the family, waved his straw boater to them. They then visited Dublin, after which, finding the weather too inclement for a voyage round Ireland, they chose instead to go round the north of Scotland and thus back to Gravesend. William got on quietly with his parliamentary work and read *David Copperfield*, while the rest of the family enjoyed the novelty of the ship.

The cruise in the Pembroke Castle was arranged at short notice, for in September 1883, it was thought by the family that it would be beneficial for the much harassed Prime Minister. The Pembroke Castle was the largest ship of the Union Castle Line, and had very recently been launched.

Donald Currie asked Mary to draw up a guest list for the Pembroke Castle. As well as her parents and herself, Herbert was free to go. Indeed, it was felt that at least two of the family were needed to look after their parents, especially Catherine, who was becoming increasingly vague and distraught. Willy and Helen had arranged to go to Switzerland on a climbing holiday, which was their glory; they would have found the Pembroke Castle constricting. Arrangements were made for Algernon West, who was representing the cabinet,

Sir Arthur Gordon, Lord Dalhousie, and Dr. Andrew Clark, who was bringing his wife, to come. Above all, Mary strove to invite some person of eminence who could make stimulating conversation with her father. Sir William Harcourt, the Home Secretary, said he and his son would be pleased to join the ship on the west coast of Scotland and go as far as Tobermoray on Mull. This would only take an afternoon, and the cruise would probably be for a week. Mary then asked Dr. Henry Scott Holland, a tutor at Oxford renowned for his preaching, but he replied:-

> It would have been immense fun, as you say, if only it had been on dry land! Why do these ships go to sea? They are most fascinating things in themselves: so bright and clean and gay. They spoil it all by going on the water.

Time was short, she had only a week to make the arrangements, and now the correspondence had to be by telegram both ways. She decided to be bold and to ask Alfred Tennyson if he would like to come. The family knew the Tennysons well, but they had not seen each other much in recent years. It was short notice but the cruise sounded delightful, and Tennyson accepted saying that he and his wife, and their son, Hallam, would come.

The cruise was looked upon as convalescence for William who had been poorly, and the papers stated had only taken carriage exercise recently. That is to say he had taken fresh air by going out for carriage drives, though of course he was tempted to take walks occasionally. The *Morning Post*, told how a policeman on duty at Hawarden heard footsteps at midnight and had 'rushed forward and rudely seized the intruder, but was agreeably surprised to discover the Premier taking late exercise.'[1]

The family party set off on September 8th. At Chester station there was excitement at meeting up with the Tennyson family, and with plenty of porters to carry the luggage, the holiday makers settled into a specially reserved saloon carriage. The greatest advantage of having a saloon carriage was that they did not have to change trains. There were comfortable seats and ample luggage space, and above all there was 'a Little Room.' Another advantage might have been privacy, but at every station when the train drew to a halt the Gladstones and the Tennysons were recognised and waved to. The saloon carriage was attached to the Manchester express as far as Carnforth, and then joined to another train going westwards to Barrow-in-Furness.

As they alighted from the train there was a crowd of onlookers surrounding the dock. The Pembroke Castle, looking immense and truly magnificent, was as yet a way off. It was necessary to board a tug-boat, the Walney, to reach the big steamer, which was well outside the harbour. There was a howling gale that played havoc with hats and dresses, and distressed Tennyson, who was dressed in his usual black cloak and big-brimmed hat.

The Pembroke Castle was the biggest as well as the newest of the Union Castle fleet, being of 4,000 tons, and 400 feet long. She was built to take passengers to South Africa, but due to Admiralty requirements could also be used for troops and light armaments. For her maiden voyage she took a double crew even though she had so few passengers. Donald Currie, who was on board to act as host to his visitors, suggested the same route as they had followed in the Grandtully Castle three years before, but omitting Dublin so as to shorten the trip. He planned that they should go north by the Hebrides, round Scotland and return by the east coast to London. They had all experienced channel steamers before but had expected the Pembroke Castle, being so big, would be steady. Sadly, it was impossible to relax and enjoy the cruise because with the appalling weather the ship pitched and rolled, despite her size. They sailed northwards, and dropped anchor at Ramsey Bay in the Isle of Man at eight o'clock. At six the next morning she moved off again. The sea was still very rough, and the holiday makers felt disillusioned, for they had anticipated strolling round the ship's decks, making enlightening conversation, and reading books they had brought with them. Mary with difficulty persuaded Tennyson to read some of his poetry, but it was not a success, for 'reading is extremely difficult and so interrupted.'

They reached Oban and picked up Sir William Harcourt and Lulu, his son, aged twenty, and missed them when they dropped them at Tobermory on the island of Mull. Here Dr. Andrew Clark and Mrs. Clark joined them. He was a serious and shrewd Scot, and it must have seemed at this stage to Mary and Herbert, who felt responsible for the arrangements, that the party was hardly going to be lighthearted.

Then, quite suddenly, the weather changed, and as the great ship made her way along the coast between the Hebridean islands everyone on board began to feel better. They passed between Skye and the mainland and docked in Loch Hourn for a night, and then edged through the narrow straits of the Kyle of Lochalsh. It was all that the heart could desire; the scenery was breath-taking and the steamer was luxurious. Donald Currie noticed, as did everybody else, that the Prime Minister was really enjoying himself and the cruise was evidently doing him much good. The passage was smooth as they passed Cape Wrath in sunshine, and the weather appeared settled for the next few days. It then occurred to Donald Currie that they might go to the Orkneys and extend their cruise with a visit to the Norwegian coast, an exciting new proposal which was readily taken up. As yet, nobody guessed what lay ahead.

Reaching the Orkney Islands, the Pembroke Castle docked at Kirkwall, towering above the fishing boats. An opportunity was taken to spend a day ashore, whereupon the citizens of Kirkwall announced they wished to confer the Freedom of the City on both the grand old men, the Premier and the Poet. The Premier was seventy-three; the Poet was seventy-four. We can picture the two elderly, eminent gentlemen; both tall, lean, and grey-haired but both instantly recognisable. Moreover, whilst the Premier had come to expect crowds wherever he went, for the Poet staring people were his chief aversion. When speeches were called for Tennyson growled ferociously that nothing would induce him to make a speech. This was often his way. He liked to be cajoled and persuaded, and graciously give way. However, the Premier was not a man to waste time and told the Poet he would include both their thanks. He started on his speech and alluded with discernment and carefully chosen words to the eternal influence of the poet in comparison with that of the politician. Unfortunately Tennyson was noticeably irritated at being taken at his word.

The Pembroke Castle then left for the longest part of the cruise across sea to the Norwegian coast. Mary and Herbert decided to get together a concert for everyone's amusement performed by the passengers for the sailors. The performers were to be first Donald Currie, Liberal M.P. for Perth, owner of the ship and an admirable host; William, a Prime Minister on holiday, and Catherine who needed a break (as she would have said) quite as much; Herbert, M.P. for Leeds and Mary, who acted as social secretary and was a born organiser; two cousins, Constance Gladstone and Albert Lyttelton; Laura Tennant, sister of Margo (Asquith), who was vivacious and kept a diary of the holiday; the dour and bearded Dr. Andrew Clark, Algernon West, previously the Principal Private Secretary, Sir Arthur Gordon and Lord Dalhousie. And, of course, the revered Mr. Tennyson, Poet Laureate who was to receive his peerage the following year. His wife, Emily, was a warm and welcoming person, like Catherine, and for that matter like Mrs. Clark — though she was not very much in evidence — a truly professional wife. Their son, Hallam, found much of his time taken up with his famous father as, of course, did Herbert.

The concert for the sailors, 'full of fun,' no doubt included music hall songs, and probably Mary, who was a brilliant pianist, organised a chorus and persuaded all the passengers to join in. Only Tennyson, who could not abide noise, tactfully excused himself by complaining he was deaf, and chose to stay out on the deck. Here he became enraptured watching the sea in the moonlight, the beauty of which he later described to Mary as 'like a great river rushing to the City of God!'

The plan was to dock at Bergen, but as there was much fog, and unease because the ship was new, orders were given to proceed to Christiana (Oslo), where they stopped a night before continuing to Copenhagen. The peaceful part of the holiday then came to an abrupt end.

When the Pembroke Castle arrived at Copenhagen there were already forty-one yachts packed into the harbour. The King and Queen of Denmark had a family gathering for the summer holidays, and royalty was there in force. When the newcomers got ashore they caused a commotion, especially the sight of the totally unexpected British Prime Minister.

The next day, Mr. Vaughan, Minister to the British Legation, boarded the Pembroke Castle. He called with an invitation to dinner with the King and Queen at Fredensburg. It was soon decided that all would accept, though later Algy West declined; quite unexpectedly he found a job of mammoth proportions on his hands, organising return invitations. The carriages provided drove through country for two hours to reach Fredensburg, an immense palace. It was, however, a happy, informal family home. The guests waiting in the drawing room, heard loud laughter and many footsteps as the royal grandchildren, seventeen of them, burst through the door. They were followed by a sight our friends from the Pembroke Castle could never forget: the King and Queen of Denmark, King Christian IX and Queen Louise; the Czar and Czarina, Emperor Alexander III and Empress Dagmar; the King and Queen of Greece, King George I and Queen Olga, and the Princess of Wales and her three daughters. Other relations, friends, and courtiers followed, until finally eighty people sat down together to dinner. Afterwards the family informality of Fredensburg was only too evident when the children performed gymnastics. Mary noted in her diary:-

. . . . great simplicity of life . . . .Music during dinner, and after we talked to all the royalties in turn, and watched the children's capital gymnastics.

A return invitation was inevitable and the next day some forty-eight guests arrived for lunch on the Pembroke Castle. These were the King and Queen of Denmark; the Crown Prince and Princess and their three sons; the King and Queen of Greece and their three sons; the Princess of Wales and one son and three daughters; the Czar and Czarina and their son and two daughters. The Crown Prince, the King of Greece, the Princess of Wales and the Czarina were all children of the King and Queen of Denmark. There were numerous other royal persons. Excitement mounted at the sight of the great state barges, richly painted and with fringed canopies, coming from the Russian and Danish yachts, and being rowed towards the big ship. Also invited were the British Minister and his wife; the British Secretary, Mr. Gosling and his wife and the two Miss Goslings; the Danish Minister of Marine, the head of the Danish navy, and three Danish admirals, all in full dress.

The first person to disappear from the reception was the Czar, flamboyantly magnificent in his uniform. Even before the Danish admirals, he made a dash to explore the new ship and see her engines. Afterwards Algy West commented:-

Never was there such an assembly of royalties on a ship before. They had not been on board three minutes when the Czar disappeared, having as I afterwards ascertained, got hold of the engineer and gone to examine every part of the ship and her machinery.[2]

After lunch there were speeches, Mr. Gladstone proposing the toasts. The King of Denmark then replied in English and the Czar in French. By this time everybody present was in a jovial mood. Algy West felt so fagged out with the worry of making the seating arrangements that he did not sit down to lunch himself but, as he put it, kept in the background. Out of sight he was not out of ear-shot and heard the Czar say, no doubt with a smile, that he would rather be King of Denmark with its pleasant proprietors, than Czar of all the Russias! Afterwards, when Algy put in an appearance the Princess of Wales came up and asked him where he had been; she introduced him to the King of Greece. He then watched the Princess join a group asking Tennyson to read some of his poetry. With gestures the poet remonstrated.

> After luncheon it was proposed that Tennyson should read something, and on his saying that one man could lead a horse to the water but ten couldn't make him drink, the Princess of Wales said, 'Oh, but I can,' and led him up to the little smoking room, where, surrounded by all these crowned heads, with his great wide-awake on his head, he read *The Grandmother*.[3]

Mary peeped round the door of the tiny smoking room to see Tennyson happily sitting between the sisters, the Czarina and Princess Alexandra. Mary wore her black velvet with jewellery she had borrowed from Laura. She flew off to tell her friend that Tennyson was sitting in his favourite big corner seat and was patting his two ladies 'just as he does us.'[4] A little pat on the arm or on the knee, and possibly a little pat under the chin at the end of a stanza?

The party on the ship then ended, the company leaving in the royal barges with a good deal of merriment. 'All the guests quitted the Pembroke Castle at 2.30 p.m. amid a salute from the guns and loud cheers from the crowd assembled on the Quay.'[5]

The ceremonies over, the holiday drawing to a close, the Pembroke Castle returned to England. She first stopped at Aldeburgh, then docked at Gravesend, where the travellers took the train to Charing Cross. William, accompanied by Albert Lyttelton, walked off to Downing Street. We can imagine the two top-hatted men striding off, the curate trying to keep up with his uncle. Catherine and Mary took a cab and Herbert supervised the luggage. The rest of the party soon dispersed. They had agreed to present the ship's officers with a piece of plate as a token of thanks, and Tennyson was asked to supply a verse, which he did. Though brief, it was very much to the point:-

> Grateful guests to gracious host,
> To and from the Danish coast.

Meanwhile news of the arrival of the British Premier at Copenhagen had been recorded in newspapers in Paris, Vienna, Berlin, and St. Petersburg, and so the news reached London. The Prussian Minister at Copenhagen was recalled from his holiday, and must have very annoyed to find all was well and there was no scandal, and thus no need for him to return. The newspaper in Berlin recorded his feelings:-

> The journal declared that if Mr. Gladstone's visit to Copenhagen had no political object the

British Premier was reckless in giving grounds for foolish speculations and for the disturbance of public opinion.

The *Morning Post*, the very essence of Conservatism, could not resist a leader of abuse. By now it was evident that the nature of the cruise was an argument enjoyed by many:-

> It is quite idle to say that Mr. Gladstone, 'like any other man,' is free to do what he likes with his holidays. So long as Mr. Gladstone holds the position of official head of the British Government his conduct cannot be judged by vague comparisons with 'any other man,' and the party organs which venture this defence of the Premier's light-headed behaviour are fully aware that there is no parallel possible between what an ordinary Cook's tourist can do and what the Premier of England ought to do.

The Queen soon got to hear of the affair — Her Majesty particularly disliked the Danish royal family — and felt indignant. Her Prime Minister had left the shores without Her Majesty's permission and, not finding him available for punishment, she wrote before his return to the Foreign Secretary, Lord Granville:-

> . . . . her unfeigned astonishment at Mr. Gladstone's want of all knowledge apparently of what is due to the Sovereign he serves.

Who would have thought that a two-week sea cruise would have lead to the Premier getting the greatest scolding of his life from the Queen? The chastisement hurt but was bravely taken, but fortunately Lord Granville, the most diplomatic person, was able to disperse the thunder-cloud that had suddenly burst over this idyllic holiday. Seventeen years earlier he had got his friend out of giving a dinner for the opposition by simply saying what he had observed — 'Mr. Gladstone is having his house painted!'

The truth this time was even stranger. As Herbert wrote, 'At Copenhagen, by pure accident, we met an extraordinary assembly of royalties.' In defending his father, he pointed out that none of the party had got permission to leave the territorial waters, and they were therefore all culpable. 'We were guiltlessly forgetful — not excluding the Poet Laureate himself.'[6]

22

The Sunbeam

In 1885 the Conservatives were back in power, and the family hurriedly packed up and left Downing Street in June. Fortunately, they were invited by a wealthy Liberal friend to stay in his house in Richmond Terrace which was just the other side of Whitehall, then a street of shoddy shops and houses. William and Catherine both looked as if they needed a holiday far away from the turmoil of political life. The ex-premier said he wanted to retire: he had already retired in 1874, and then led the government the last five years. When the Queen noted that he did not look well she asked her doctor, Sir William Jenner, for a report on his health. He in turn asked Sir Andrew Clark, (he had recently received a knighthood), who decided to confide what he had said in a letter to Catherine:-

> 16 Cavendish Square,
> W.
> July 18, 1885.

Dear Mrs. Gladstone,

    Last night Sir William Jenner came to me with a message from the Queen desiring to be informed of Mr. Gladstone's health. I thought it best to reply 'offhand' without appearing to require previous consultation. I said that I had made no professional examination; that with the exception of some hoarseness caused by undue exercise of voice in conversation Mr. Gladstone was in good health, but that he appeared grave and full of anxious thought. These, as literally as I can reconvey them were the exact words I used in replying to Sir William Jenner. Thinking it my duty to acquaint you with what passed I have troubled you with this note which needs no answer.

    Yours sincerely,
    Andrew Clark.[1]

At the beginning of August William and Catherine with Mary and Herbert stayed with Baron Ferdinand de Rothschild at Waddesden Manor, near Aylesbury. They found the extreme luxury oppressive, and Mary could not understand how a house with such expensive furniture had only thirty bad French novels in the way of books. Herbert was called upon to speak for his father who had completely lost his voice. For the family were never left alone for long, and when a deputation of a hundred local Liberals called, Herbert, ready to comply though hardly enjoying such a task, gave thanks on behalf of his father. The Liberals 'expressed a hope that he would speedily be restored to health and again lead the Liberal party to victory.'[2] Were their hopes to be fulfilled? They were.

142

First of all, a solution had to be found for the lost voice. Sir Thomas Brassey says in his book, *The Sunbeam*: 'In 1885, as a remedy for a temporary 'extinction de voix' Mr. Gladstone was advised to try a sea voyage.' The voyage of the Sunbeam was then arranged, though it now seems as strange cure for an elderly man, crossing the North Sea and visiting Norway, the country of precipitous mountains. The Sunbeam had much more movement when the sea was rough than the Pembroke Castle, being about an eighth of the size. Mary commented:-

. . . . the maximum of tossing we had on the Pembroke Castle was the minimum on the nicely graceful little Sunbeam.

When Catherine opened a bazaar in aid of the London Sailors' Society, she mentioned she had been on a delightful trip on the Pembroke Castle. Perhaps, as well as the usual pink glow of her cheeks there was a twinkle in the eye, hinting that it had not been delightfully smooth all the time, for she spoke with feeling of the hazards of the sea. The sailors were so touched that they afterwards presented her with a model of the ship.

The voyage on the Sunbeam took place two years after the cruise on the Pembroke Castle, and though the route was similar the two ships were quite different, the Sunbeam being a privately owned yacht. The owner was Sir Thomas Brassey, Liberal M.P. for Hastings. His father had amassed a fortune as a railway contractor, having built the South-Western Railway and even built a short tract of railway in the Crimea to move armaments and supplies. Thomas Brassey's passion was the sea. He was founder of Brassey's Naval Annual and had been Financial Secretary to the Admiralty, where his responsibilities lay with the manning of the Navy and the Naval Reserve. During the voyage he envisaged an opportunity to unburden himself with an explanation of Admiralty accounts. He asked the private secretary, the cheerful George Leveson-Gower to talk to the man at the top, but by that time they were on the high seas and George persuaded him to leave it alone. George later referred to it as 'some trifling muddle over Admiralty finance,'[3] but readers of *Punch* were told it was a 'little slip of half a million.' In any case it was holiday time and the personalities on the yacht felt they needed a change of scene, and they were going to get it.

The Sunbeam was exquisitely built with every possible luxury. She had been designed by Mr. St. Clare Byrne of Liverpool, and completed in 1874. Her displacement tonnage was 531 tons, and her engines developed a speed of 10.3 knots at an average daily consumption of four tons. She was a three-masted schooner, iron framed and with a teak skin, a perfect ocean going cruiser devised with no expense spared. She was to be the forerunner of modern luxury yachts, and the cost of running her must have been phenomenal. The Brasseys set the style for other yacht owners, and by the eighteen-eighties the Sunbeam's name had become a household word.

She was the first steam yacht to circumnavigate the world purely for the pleasure of achievement, and had caused a sensation on her return. What was so remarkable was that the Brasseys always travelled as a family. Thomas Brassey was a very experienced skipper and looked the part. Thick set with sloping shoulders, his cap pulled well down over his weather-beaten brow, he thought little of staying up two or three nights at a time to steer his beloved yacht if he felt it necessary. He and Anna were of the same mind. She knew the safe passage of the Sunbeam depended on his knowledge and skill, and he later realised the ultimate success was due to her sheer determination and perseverance. They were both physically very strong; what he had in stamina she had in pace, for she was never still.

Anna Brassey always kept a diary and later wrote articles and books on their travels. She would sit in the yacht at her exquisite writing desk in the corner of her room on her pretty button-backed chair, dipping her quill pen into the heavy unspillable inkpot. Around her were pictures, pot plants in heavy brass holders, little statues of her children and various decorative cases. Above her fitted corner desk of mahogany with brass fittings was an enclosed shelf and a pretty rural scene. Draped brocade curtains, held back with encrusted braids, kept out any draughts or shielded sun.

When the Sunbeam was new they first explored the British Isles, then the Mediterranean, then across to Canada, and later Australia. On their world voyage they took their three girls, Mabelle, Muriel, and Marie, the youngest and still a toddler. Tab, their son, travelled as far as Rio de Janeiro, and then returned to school at Harrow. Tab's proper name was Allnut — his mother had been a Miss Allnut — but he preferred to be called by his initials. They also took a doctor and an artist, Mr. Bingham, and Anna had engravings made of his sketches for her books.

Above all, Tom and Anna Brassey were intrepid as were their children. Near the start of the voyage round the world when Mabelle, aged about ten, was almost swept overboard, she simply said to her mother, 'I did not think at all, Mamma, but felt sure we were gone!' When Anna wanted to view a coral island from above so as to see the lagoon in the South Seas, near Tahiti, she was hoisted up the mast and Tom climbed up to join her. She described the event in her book, *A Voyage in the Sunbeam, our Home on the Ocean for Eleven Months*:

> After lunch, Tom had me hoisted up to foretop mast-head in a 'boatswain's chair,' which is simply a small plank, suspended by ropes at the four corners, and used by the men to sit on when they scrape the masts. I was very carefully secured with a rope tied round my petticoats and gently hoisted up . . . . but once I got accustomed to the smallness of the seat, the airiness of my perch, and the increased roll of the vessel, I found my position by no means an unpleasant one. Tom climbed up the rigging and joined me shortly afterwards.

For the Gladstone's cruise departure date was fixed for August 8th, and the voyage was planned to last for three weeks. In the morning the family attended the christening of Willy's only son at St. George's, Hanover Square, and 'the late Prime Minister looked far from well. Mrs. Gladstone wore a dress of dark purple blue and bonnet to match.'[4] Then to Charing Cross station, and by six William, Catherine and Mary were on the Sunbeam which was speeding down the Thames with a fresh wind from the south-west, taking up full sail.

Whenever possible the sails were used, otherwise the fireman would make up the boiler if steam was needed, although sailing was no economy: the consumption of coal was much less expensive than the wear and tear of the costly sails and ropes, which became more torn flapping about in a calm than in a stiff breeze. The thirty-six hour crossing was rough at times and never smooth for one moment. Sir Thomas Brassey noted in his diary:-

> August 10th. Blowing hard. Mr. Gladstone, by keeping quiet in his cabin, was not at all uncomfortable, much to the satisfaction of Sir Andrew Clark.

In truth all the passengers, except the Brassey family, were being tortured by the miserable tossing about. Catherine remarked that William had not been sick, rather inferring that the rest of them had. She kept to her bunk, and even that at times was difficult. She described her agony in an effort to stay put: 'I had to make plain as to the very sticking in bed for often I might, with the sudden pitch of the boat, be thrown out, bodily out!'[5]

Meanwhile Mary kept a note on how often she was sick. The Sunbeam's passenger accommodation was full and George Leveson-Gower, a cousin of Willy's wife and the tallest of the secretaries in Downing Street, was given a seaman's cabin. He kept cracking his head on the cupboard fixed just above the pillow every time he turned over in bed. he soon became conditioned to move his head only sideways, and found this habit carried on after he had got home.

On reaching the Norwegian coast at Stavanger Tom was up at 4 a.m. to take on a pilot, a man he already knew; the Brasseys had been here nine years before. The yacht was anchored, and after breakfast the passengers rowed ashore to a welcome that must have taken them by surprise. The scene is best described by Tom:-

> Our reception on landing was impressive. From early morning groups of townspeople had been hovering about the quays trying to get a glimpse of the well-renowned statesman. I steered our heavily-laden gig to the landing place, where Mr. and Mrs. Gladstone received a cordial and enthusiastic welcome. Bare-headed spectators lined the streets. Every window and doorway was filled with onlookers; flags had been hoisted everywhere. Church bells were ringing. It was touching to see Mr. Gladstone walking up the narrow street, his hat almost constantly raised in response to perpetual salutations.[6]

The Sunbeam then sailed northwards and entered the Hardanger Fiord. The fields were green, the corn was cut, and brightly-coloured wooden houses dotted the banks and hillsides. There was no more perfect way to see the fiords than from the Sunbeam, 'fairy-like, with sails set and everything spotless white.' Even Mary began to be glad she had come. The next morning she got up early in her dressing gown to go on deck and watch Anna with Muriel and Marie, aged thirteen and ten, dive into the sea. She was amazed at their bathing dresses: 'they wear next to nothing, scarlet tight-fitting trousers and small tight bodices reaching to above their arms with no sleeves!' Anna wore a similar bathing dress in bright stripes, 'a most unattractive object.' Watching Anna and her two little fish plunge off the yacht was entertaining enough but what really amused her was the look on Sir Andrew Clark's face. He wore an expression of complete astonishment as the uninhibited bathers bounced around him. Meanwhile Catherine was enjoying a cold bath:-

. . . . we have a bath at hand of sea water!! Indulged this morning after oh, such a night of real repose and capital sleep — the sense of relief from that miserable tossing about.[7]

One hopes that everybody slept soundly the next night too, though weather conditions meant an early start. The party had been ashore to visit a Mr. Walters, who like many of the British came to Norway for the superb salmon fishing, and it was he who gave the alarm:-

At an early hour came a knock at the cabin door. Kindred, our sailing master, addressing Tom in a very doleful voice, said, 'Please, sir, I want to get up some steam, as her stern is touching the shore. We were on deck in a few moments, and there, to our dismay, found the Sunbeam lying almost broadside on to a rocky beach. The situation had fortunately been observed from the shore by Mr. Walters, who sent a hawser to keep the vessel's bow from touching the ground. When at last the steam was up we made another attempt to anchor. The wind was too strong and we were reluctantly compelled to heave up again and proceed to Odde in search of better shelter.

The weather was constantly changing and the scenery truly breathtaking. As each head of the fiord was explored to its furthest point, the passage became narrower and the banks more precipitous. Long expeditions were made to view the Hardanger, known as the most romantic of the fiords, from above, and to see the Buerbrae glacier and the waterfalls of Laatefos and Skarsfos.

All the passengers could now enjoy themselves. As well as the five Brasseys and the three Gladstones, there were five other passengers. Sir Andrew Clark, Arnold Morley (a satellite), and two young men: George Leveson-Gower and Lulu Harcourt. Also Mrs. Bridge, the wife of an admiral whom she had not seen for four years, who sang delightfully in the evenings. There was, of course, a grand piano on the ship, and Mary was always in demand as a pianist. Sometimes a sailor would play the fiddle or accordion and there would be a singsong. Or there would be readings from famous authors: George chose the court scene from the *Pickwick Papers* which made everyone laugh. In a letter home Catherine commented:-

Our party is really a success. Sir A. Clark with good talk chimes in with Papa and Sir T. Brassey as to many interesting talks, amongst others some very scientific, including the Dee and the Mersey!

The Sunbeam was built to carry forty-three persons. The crew consisted of a sailing master, a boatswain and signalman; two engineers, two fireman, a carpenter and nine able seaman. The able seaman were paid thirty shillings a week, and were expected to supply their own food. A staff of six looked after the passengers, that is to say they had to clean, launder and tidy; also to wait at table. Each had certain duties under the Chief Steward, who had charge of the store room. These were the deck-house steward, the bedroom steward, and a mess-room boy. There was a lady's maid and a children's maid. There was a cook and a cook's boy for the passengers, and another cook and cook's boy for below deck. The cooks and stewards were paid around £2 a week, and the skippers and engineers £3-£4 a week with their food supplied. There were also two sailors for the gig, a large rowing boat, and one in charge of the lifeboat cutter. There was also a steam launch and a dingy which were used occasionally.

Sundays were always observed. The Bishop of Durham and his two chaplains who were staying in the vicinity came abroad for early service; morning service was at the hotel, and evening service on the Sunbeam again when many visitors attended. In between some of the party visited the Norwegian church:-

The rector of the parish was preaching his last sermon to his flock previous to his departure to another district. In his black gown and white ruff he presented a striking appearance, standing out in strong relief from the white background. On one side of the church sat the women and girls; on the other the men and boys. The discourse of the minister, a grave, earnest-looking man with reddish hair and closely cut beard, must have been of a stirring character. Among the women there was scarcely a dry eye. The church, which is probably capable of holding four or five hundred people, was so crowded that it was difficult to find places

The next day the Bishop of Durham and his two chaplains were back, this time to join a ten-hour expedition, arriving on the Sunbeam at 5 a.m. After a short steam they all set off in 'cockle-shell' boats in fierce wind and rain before starting on their nine-mile walk and climb over rough ground. Narrow bridges crossed the treacherous gulleys of swirling torrents rushing down from the mountains, which looked to be near-vertical. Some of the ladies rode ponies. Mary did not like the constant lurching but had the obliging George to lead her pony. Seeing her father approach a bridge without a handrail, Mary said to him: 'Run quick George, his head is so bad, run and get on the precipice side of him, quickly.' Understandably George hesitated before catching up the man who was the fastest walker and always out in front. She afterwards discovered that he himself had a bad head for heights. Another pony carried panniers containing a sumptuous picnic. Mary noted:-

We did enjoy luncheon. I remember the dismay of the Bishop's countenance when he found the apricot puffs and the raspberry roly-poly were finished, and its corresponding gleam when jam on a biscuit was suggested.

There were fishing expeditions, and wherever they went the Brasseys seemed fearless, and not to worry for their guests: 'Mr. Harcourt was the most successful of the party. He landed a large fish after a tremendous struggle at the top of the weir, down which we momentarily expected him to disappear.' Lulu (later Viscount Harcourt) also enjoyed taking photos of people, though they had to stand still with great patience. Anna Brassey successfully photographed views of the landscape. Back through the beautiful fiord and a short stop at Bergen, where they were greeted with the short little Norwegian 'hurrah,' the ex-British Consul wanted to give a banquet, but Tom though it safer to turn down the invitation after the dire consequences that had followed the luncheon on the Pembroke Castle.

Then further up the coast to visit the Sogne fiord. As the Sunbeam proceeded, it became more and more difficult to navigate and more dangers arose. They stopped at Gudvengen where the houses cling to the ledges of the mountain like an eagle's nest and the children had to be tied by ropes for fear of falling. The village was illuminated in honour of the well-known yacht whilst moonlight showed up the summits of the mountains. It was an unforgettable experience. They drove up the Romsdal valley, then sailed to Molde, before setting off for the Shetland Islands. No sooner were plans made than there was a delay, for the Osborne had arrived carrying the Prince of Wales. He was in great spirits and enormously enthusiastic over Norway, and called to see his friends on the Sunbeam, inviting everyone to the Osborne to dinner. It was, of course, a much larger yacht and had none of the fairy-like quality and exquisite taste of the furnishings of the Sunbeam, but the Prince was charming and there were fresh strawberries.

Later that evening they set sail homewards with Tom at the helm. At first there was a light breeze, and by midnight they were under full sail. The passengers found it very rough as they continued sailing the next day. A fall in the barometer predicted a coming storm and it was decided to make for the Scottish coast and abandon the visit to the Shetlands. With the Orkneys in sight they made for Thurso, and no sooner had they anchored than a message came: would Mr. Gladstone come and give a speech? Catherine did not hesitate to give a polite refusal, but within a short while a rowing boat was seen with the Provost of Thurso and other important townspeople who gave a formal address, and then had a chance to talk with the man they felt would listen to their problems.

Losing no time after this they sailed down the east coast and into the Moray Firth, spending the night for sentimental reasons at Dingwall, where William's mother had been born and brought up; her father had been Provost of Dingwall. Off again at 3 a.m. they made for Inverness under steam. The Gladstones were pressed for time, not for reasons of business but because William's eldest brother was celebrating his golden wedding, and they did not wish to miss the occasion. They knew that they could catch the mail train if they got off the ship at Fort George. In the very early hours there was a curious scene wherein the three Gladstones shook hands and thanked every member of the crew. They then piled into a fly, a one-horse cab, for the four mile drive to the station. They caught the mail train to Aberdeen, took another one to Laurencekirk and got to Fasque. There they met up happily with Helen who was staying with Tom and Louisa's big family.

Only the last lap of the journey remained, a long day in the train to North Wales. At home they found Harry and Herbert, and were soon to see Willy and Gerty and their three small children at the Red House, and Stephy and Annie at the Rectory. But nobody demonstrated appreciation for the return of her master more than Petz, the big, black Pomeranian, who positively vibrated with pleasure.

The best part of many a holiday is getting home, but home routine and tranquillity were soon to be disturbed. The five Brasseys had been invited to stay, and come they did. As well as a large house in Sussex they also had a place in Cheshire, as for relaxation they rode to hounds with unflagging energy. Tom and Anna and their three girls made their presence felt by their ceaseless energy; and in the evenings, when everybody else was ready for bed, they would be laughing with crossword puzzles and paper games, bringing back happy reminiscences of the voyage to Norway on the Sunbeam.

23
Dollis Hill

The custom amongst those who could afford a town house and a country house was to pass most of the year in the country, and to spend the season: May, June, and July in London. This gave those in society an opportunity to meet at balls and receptions, and simply by paying afternoon calls at the conventional time of between three and five. When Sundays came round many wished for a day of relaxation.

On a brief visit to Osborne in June 1872, Catherine noted:-

I never hear the Queen talk without feeling one ought to be the better for it, perfectly natural and simple because she is so true. The Queen seemed to take great interest in my husband's rest. Turning to me, 'You like him to be out of London on Sundays.' I answered I wish Her Majesty would lay command upon this.

In London the pavements and parks were full of a mass of humanity making the most of their one free day of the week. The streets were not as crowded as on weekdays but there was still non-stop traffic, and the noise, dirt, and smells made those who knew the peace and quiet of the countryside long to be there.

It was in those extremely hot summers of the eighteen-eighties, often referred to as 'dog-days,' that some of the very wealthy set about having what would now be called a week-end cottage and what was then a fair-sized house on the outskirts of London as it was then, say in Streatham, Wimbledon or Hampstead, where the heath was common land and the gravel pits had recently been filled in to make agreeable ponds.

The house William and Catherine went to in the eighteen-eighties for Sundays was Littleberries in Mill Hill, some twelve miles north of Downing Street. Here they were guests of the Marquis and Marchioness of Aberdeen who, though of an age to be their children, had become increasingly close friends. They had rented Littleberries, which was a delightful late-medieval house built for Nell Gwynne by Charles II, a fact constantly in dispute amongst visitors as they strolled on the grass terraces down to the summer house at the bottom of the garden. Before long the occasional Sunday spent at Littleberries became every Sunday during the summer, then Sunday night was added, then Saturday night as well. For a long time the term weekend was not invented, but be called simply 'Saturday till Monday.'

After three years of renting Littleberries the Aberdeens decided to purchase a house not so far out of London. They looked in the direction of Hampstead, and managed to find a farm and a delightfully situated farmhouse called Dollis Hill, and they had no hesitation in deciding to buy the property. It was not until some years later that the Aberdeens invested in farming in Canada with such disastrous results that they had to curtail their expenses. Dollis Hill was then in the depths of the country, the house surrounded by an orchard.

The address at the time was simply Dollis Hill, Kilburn, and William and Catherine were pressed to stay by the Aberdeens who seemed to revere them. They would drive from Downing Street towards Marble Arch and up the Edgware Road, up the hill to the old village of Kilburn and then along a winding mud road up Shooters Hill and through rolling countryside to reach Dollis Hill. The farm then covered 500 acres. The house, the garden and the park remain today open to the public, but the fields were built over in the nineteen-thirties. Supplies for the household came from the kitchen garden and farm, or from Kilburn, the nearest village. It was observed by some that the man who had spoken against the idea of people retreating to the country for Saturday-till-Mondays because it parted parents from their children, had changed his mind. Often members of the Gladstone and Lyttelton families would be invited to spend the Sunday at Dollis Hill.

Throughout his life William had frequent illnesses and accidents. In 1880 he nearly died of typhoid, and in February 1881 returning from a late-night sitting he slipped and badly cut his head open. The alarm spread round London in a flash, and Mary, who was at a party at Lord Rosebery's house came home as quickly as she knew how by travelling by herself in a growler. It was past midnight and her father had been carried into the butler's bedroom next to the front door, and the housekeeper was out of bed holding a candle for the doctor to stop the flow of blood from her father's head:-

His shirt was all over blood, and the scene in Hyam's bedchamber with Mrs. Hampton like Lady Macbeth with a candle and nightcap, doctor plastering up head, was very dramatic

Fortunately, as was his usual form, William soon recovered, but the weekends spent at Dollis were a great help in retaining his strength and vitality. Ishbel Aberdeen and Catherine started their very close friendship when Ishbel exchanged confidences when she was having her first baby. They kept closely in touch and when they did not meet wrote often. Catherine had known Ishbel's parents, named Marjoribanks, and Ishbel remained close to her mother and frequently had photo-copies of Catherine's letters made to send to her. On the one hand photo-copies were preferable for anyone who could afford them than a copy in somebody else's handwriting; on the other hand a certain amount of guessing was needed to interpret Catherine's writing.

Later Ishbel persuaded Catherine to become President of the Women's Liberal Federation. Certainly the majority of Liberal members of parliament were not keen for women to have the vote because they realised that this would apply only to women who were owners of property, who would mostly be Conservative. When in 1892 William finally agreed to speak to the annual meeting of the W.L.F. he suffered a sudden bout of influenza and failed to appear, which seemed to the female audience as more than a coincidence.

The Sundays at Dollis were very quiet, attending church and going for walks. There were never any games on Sundays, no tennis, no billiards, and definitely no card games. With the improvement in the train service, Lord and Lady Rosbery asked Herbert for a Saturday till Monday at Mentmore. He was returning to London on Monday morning when two elderly men boarded the train at Watford. He was becoming increasingly annoyed at the far-fetched accusations people were making about his father which infuriated him, yet on reflexion sometimes seemed funny and made a good story to tell. This time the two men sat opposite and talked of the government, and gradually the conversation became more extravagant and exaggerated. Things were in a pretty sorry state they agreed and the Liberals must be to blame. Herbert knew what would come up next and he did not have to wait long: a malicious remark attributed to his father. At first he was tickled: here was an occasion when he could listen incognito to the prittle-prattle, but the two men were both elderly and this was a time when the views of the elderly were expected to be respected. As the train sped on the remarks became more extreme. Herbert no longer thought it funny, but he felt it best to lie low.

Then came the comment 'very brutal,' and quite suddenly Herbert found himself interrupting: 'This is a public railway carriage and I must ask you not to speak disrespectfully of Mr. Gladstone.' The elderly gents looked 'thunderstruck, then became angry.' They could hardly take back what they had just said to each other, and challenged Herbert's right to speak. He replied, 'I am Mr. Gladstone's son, and I am not going to allow it.' No sooner said than the discoursers apologised profusely, and said they were sorry to speak so openly in public. The conversation now changed direction. They said, as it happened, they had always admired Mr. Gladstone's personal character and abilities, and actually went on the thank Herbert for stopping them! By the time the train had reached Euston, Herbert got up to leave, and with what he called 'stately bows' found himself insisting that he perhaps, after all, might have spoken to them too strongly.

The increase in traffic and industry and the direction the government was taking bewildered persons who found it hard to accept the rapid social change. The Crown Princess, then a widow of forty, frequently corresponded with Lady Ponsonby, wife of the Queen's Private Secretary. Both, who had been life-long Liberals, now agreed they had become 'reflecting ones.' The Crown Princess commented in her correspondence that Mr. Gladstone was 'so absorbed by the wants of the lower classes and middle class, and with the tasks of giving them all they may safely have . . . .' What worried them even more, was that they could not accept the notion of Ireland having Home Rule, like many of England's upper crust, for if this happened part of the British Empire would be lost and that to them was unthinkable. The Crown Princess wrote to Lady Ponsonby:-

Berlin, December 5th 1885.

Dearest Mary,
 . . . . What had become of us Liberals? And yet I am quite conscious of being as good a one as ever. It only shows that we are reflecting ones, and cannot, out of party feeling, rush blindly after Mr. Gladstone, or Mr. Chamberlain, especially after the latter! His doctrines are rather too raw for me and I do not think the national stomach could quite digest them . . . .[1]

Joseph Chamberlain, who headed the radical side of the Liberal party, did not favour Home Rule for Ireland: this was the issue which divided parliament and divided the people. When the Irish had bad weather for their crops they starved, and this happened in 1879, leading to great bitterness in the years that followed. To get a Bill for Home Rule through the House of Commons was hard enough, but to get it passed by the House of Lords was almost impossible, for many of them were Irish landlords. That Ireland should be divided was not considered a possible solution at the time.

Mr. Gladstone was in a hornet's nest. While he tried to take life calmly in his old age, people looked to their newspapers to find out in what direction the government was likely to move. The Manager of the National Press Agency wrote to Herbert that 'the whole party was drifting to loggerheads and that no one knew what to believe.' Herbert, who had won his seat in Leeds promising Home Rule, went to London and discussed what he should do with close colleagues. Then he called at the National Press Agency. Afterwards he said: 'My great blunder was not in giving the interview, but in not making the condition that I should see what they proposed to publish.' For soon the news was out, not only distorted and exaggerated that Ireland would be having Home Rule, but also under his father's name. Instead of being accused of what today is known as a 'leak' or being a 'mole,' Herbert was said to have 'flown the kite;' a term that meant the message had been flown in the sky to gauge the public reaction.

The Duke of Westminster[2] felt strongly that Home Rule should be delayed. He had always sent flowers from Eaton Hall for William's birthday for many years, not just a bouquet but several large boxes of flowers grown in his green houses. On December 29th 1885, no flowers were sent.

The family lost many friends. Amongst them John Bright, who often came to dinner. He had brought up Catherine's plea for better conditions in work houses amongst his colleagues and in parliament, and admired her courage. When he was ill Catherine would send him oranges, and he always wrote her a charming letter of thanks. Now when Catherine invited him to dinner he wrote:-

Euston Hotel,
June 1, 1886.

Dear Mrs. Gladstone,

Your invitation is very kind, and I wish I could freely accept it, but at this moment when I am driven into serious, but I hope only temporary opposition to Mr. Gladstone in connection with his unfortunate Irish policy, I feel as tho' my company at your table could not be as pleasant to you and as satisfactory to myself as heretofore.

You will see that I write frankly, explaining precisely why I will ask you to excuse and forgive me if I do not join you at dinner this evening.

I cannot tell you how grieved I am at the crisis at which we have arrived, but judgement and conscience must rule rather than personal preferences. As for myself, if you cannot approve, I may hope that you will be able to forgive.

Believe me very sincerely,
John Bright.[3]

24

Tegernsee

In 1885 Stephy, having been Rector of Hawarden for eleven years, married Annie Wilson, one of fourteen children of an eminent surgeon in Liverpool. By now a telephone line had been installed. In the early days a telephone was connected between two selected houses not too far away, yet far enough to be well out of shouting distance. Lucy Cavendish commented on 'this enchanting new marvel' which 'Uncle W., who is in some respects the greatest Tory out, will have nothing to say to.'

Shortly after Stephy was married, Mary married Harry Drew, a curate of Hawarden. Harry had set out to become a barrister, and was reading for the bar when, on vacation, he accompanied Henry Pierrepont to Italy as tutor. Henry was eighteen; he caught typhoid in Rome and died three weeks later. Harry Drew so agonised during the illness that he resolved to take Holy Orders if Henry recovered, and when Henry died he did not change his mind. It was whilst he was a curate at Hawarden that he met Mary, who was older than he. By then Mary had become the 'home daughter' and her parents relied upon her skill, tact and organisation of the household. After her marriage Mary stayed at home playing the part of social secretary to her parents, and Harry as well as being a curate, catalogued his father-in-law's books which went to St. Deiniol's library, now a residential library at Hawarden.

In the summer of 1886 the defeated prime minister needed to get away for a holiday incognito. The third administration had lasted from February to June, when the Home Rule for Ireland Bill was narrowly defeated. The Liberals resigned and following the July election the Conservatives were back in power. In August Helen wrote to Harry, who was in India:-

> It has been horrid for you to be away through it all. The elections were beastly at the time. People had been so hopeful, so enthusiastic that one got hopeful too, and then when it was once plain things were going against us, I longed for it to be over, and it seemed such a time before all was finished . . . .[1]

What William needed soon was a holiday to forget London and, if possible to relax in peace. Such proved to be the holiday at Villa Arco, an idyllic spot overlooking a sheltered lake surrounded by majestic mountains. Helen was asked to accompany her father to Tegernsee, which was near Munich. Catherine, also tired, preferred to stay at home, and by now the eldest four of the family were married, Harry was in India and Herbert was busy dealing with constituency business; so Helen said she would go. As was so often the way, the holiday was fixed at short notice. Villa Arco on Tegernsee, south of Munich, the nearest station, belonged to the family of Lord Acton, who travelled with William and Helen. Lord Acton had been recommended for his appointment as Professor of Modern History at Cambridge by the former, after some agonising because he was a Roman Catholic. Famous as the mastermind behind the *Cambridge Modern History*, he was an ardent Liberal and former Member of Parliament. The Queen relied upon him as the authority on her German relations. He had a large forehead, a long though thin beard, and a rather formidable sphinx-like appearance, but was always very kind to the family. He had married the daughter of his cousin who came from Bavaria, and who owned the enchanting villa at Tegernsee.

William, Helen and Lord Acton were seen off at Charing Cross station by Catherine, Herbert and some friends. They then took the ferry from Dover. It was a delightful, calm passage, the sea a 'gorgeous blue,' which the travellers wished could have lasted longer. At Calais they had a lunch of soup from the station buffet, followed by 'home food.' They had brought with them a basket containing a loaf of bread, a pot of butter, sliced meat, a lump of cheese, and fruit cake, all wrapped up in cloths; and bottles of water. Helen wrote later to Mary:-

> We have a nice first-class to ourselves, but between the red velvet and the sun it was very hot: straight on to Brussels, arriving at eight. We had roast beef, apricots and rice, and iced water for dinner, very refreshing, at the Bellevue Hotel. Then a stroll in the dark in the park, then off again at 11.00 p.m.

On a previous visit to Tegernsee in 1877, William had gone with Catherine, Mary and Herbert. Once across the channel they had travelled by carriage, which meant stopping each night, and although they had stayed in a reputable hotel in Munich, Mary had found a flea in her bed.

This time the journey by train was to take altogether two days and two nights, with a short stay in Frankfurt to break the tedious sitting in railway carriages. They chose to pass two nights in trains. Even when they set off they were all tired, and the nights were not at all comfortable, but had to be made the best of. Helen described how they managed in the carriage to Mary:-

> We packed up at once for the night. Father, by a neat arrangement with portmanteau and cushion, lying across one end, Lord Acton and I have the rest each side. Your brown shawl came in very useful to put over Father's legs. We slept a good deal I think though rather broken, so did Lord Acton. I was very proud of myself because towards the end of the night I went to sleep too.
> Lord Acton looked so uncomfortable, nothing over him except a pocket handkerchief over his head, and never lying flat down. We had whispered conversations now and then which helped time to pass.[2]

As she suffered a somewhat sleepless night Helen could at last be thankful the last few difficult months were over. It had been sad packing up pictures, books and photos in Downing Street: 'we had all got settled in so comfortably, and it is such a nice house,' but Helen described as the last straw the new paint being put on before they were out. Michael Hicks-Beach had been chosen to decorate the house and had ordered glaring red walls, which she strongly disliked. In short turning out had been 'grisely,' and the family had finally left by the garden door. All the secretaries had been sent off for their summer holidays when the government had resigned, and during July the family had to toil unaided with the correspondence which continued to pour in. During this tense period for the family Helen had been offered the appointment as the first head of Royal Holloway College, a college of the University of London, near Virginia Water, recently built and at the time considered generously endowed. She decided she preferred to stay as Vice-Principal of Newnham College, and turned the promotion down.

Eventually the night in the railway carriage turned into morning, with an opportunity to have coffee and rolls at 6 o'clock at Cologne, where they had to change trains for Frankfurt. Sleeping in the carriage overnight had enabled the ex-Prime Minister to travel unrecognised. Fortunately, apart from seeing one Newnham student on the boat, they had managed to avoid being noticed. Now reaching Frankfurt station they received a friendly smile from a tall man with penetrating eyes, though nobody else knew them. It was Willy on his way to Switzerland, who by coincidence had been on the same train. He often went in September and no doubt Helen would have given her heart to go with him. Leaving Willy they spent a night at the Hotel de Russie. It was 'piping' hot, so they relaxed on arrival and, as Helen put it: 'I have kept very quiet every since as it is so hot that even sitting still I am in a perspi.' They later had an evening drive round 'this handsome town' and called on the Consul to take tea with his ladies.

Left Frankfurt about 11 p.m. and travelled straight to Munich, where we arrived between seven and eight. The seats of the carriage were made to pull out so that we had three beds across. Even I slept a good many substantial bits, and both Father (again covered with your brown shawl) and Lord Acton slept a great deal, though broken up.

Arriving at Munich they were met by Lord Acton's two nephews and taken to the family's palace in the city for breakfast. Helen was amazed at the size of the house as a room upstairs was unlocked where she could freshen up after the night in the train. They then drove ten miles south in a carriage and four to Tegernsee, a small lake that lay beneath the Bavarian Alps, to Villa Arco.

Although called a villa because it served as a holiday house, Villa Arco was extremely large with a courtyard. There to greet them were Lady Acton and her children, and her parents who owned the villa. Also there, to William's great delight, was his old and distinguished friend, Dr. Ignaz Döllinger, for many years Professor of ecclesiastical history at Munich University. The family had nicknamed him Teeny as even in his prime he was remarkably small: he was now eighty-eight years old and had a shock of white hair, but he still bathed in the lake every morning before breakfast. William had met him in 1845, and the two had since been the closest of friends, meeting only occasionally but corresponding frequently. Dr. Döllinger was a liberal Roman Catholic who did not believe in papal infallibility, and who was excommunicated in 1870 following the Vatican Council. Lord Acton was also a Roman Catholic with similar beliefs. People never knew why he had not been excommunicated too, and of course, did not like to ask.

Lord Acton had always encouraged Mary and Helen in their serious reading. He had an extraordinary knowledge on any subject they liked to mention, and they likened him to a walking encyclopaedia. Later he became a Lord-in-Waiting to the Queen. His knowledge of the intricacies of the Royal Family's relations, especially German, was unsurpassed. Within Villa Arco German was generally spoken, but William and Helen spoke English and French. They had both brought French novels with them to read on the holiday.

One day some relations and friends came out from Munich to join the house party, and a great deal of photography went on much to everybody's amusement. Dr. Döllinger was given a deck chair which meant his feet touched the ground but his head hardly appeared above his knees in the photographs. Not surprisingly his expression was all agog, while others patiently held their breath in an effort to stay completely still. Unfortunately, these early photographs often faded very quickly.

The large white house was in a very beautiful situation, and Mary had been enchanted when she had been there. She described it in romantic terms:-

A chalet on the borders of a blue lake, steep wooded hills rising straight from the water, 6 or 7,000 feet high. Be-creepered balconies on to which we step out from all the windows, making green leaved frames to the enchanting views.

The days were spent with breakfast at 9.30, dinner at 2 o'clock, and supper at 5.30. Helen longed to go off for long walks and climbs in the hills, but they were held back because the Countess Leopoldine, who owned Villa Arco, was not a walker. When they had first arrived Helen had noticed her father's look of dismay when he saw his hostess had a train to her dress. Furthermore, Lady Acton walked tiresomely slowly, and Dr. Döllinger not only walked slowly being eighty-eight, but had a habit of stopping altogether when he spoke.

However, a climb of the hills was arranged. Dick, the Acton's son, was keen to go, and the party included cousins from Munich and two English tutors. Lord Acton stayed behind. He then had an opportunity to write to Catherine in private. She had written to tell him that Mary, living at Hawarden, had had a still-born son prematurely, and was very poorly. Mary grieved with two of her closest friends: Constance, Duchess of Westminster, and Maggie, Lady Stepney, who called to view the dead baby.

Catherine had sent her letter with George Leveson-Gower who was on holiday and had called with his father to spend a short time at Villa Arco. It seems extraordinary she did not want to worry her husband with this important personal message unless Lord Acton thought fit. Fortunately, Mary pulled through, but it appears that her father and sister did not discover the news of the calamity until they got home. Helen, who was less than two years younger than Mary and an extremely close sister, must have been particularly upset.

Meanwhile from Tegernsee Lord Acton wrote Catherine 'just a postcard,' but in such small writing and with words crammed together that it was very difficult to read. It began:-

> It is my privilege today, as they were all off to the top of a mountain, and leave me to describe their goings on. I can really say that all has gone well. I daresay Mr. Gladstone has chafed a little at the absence of political and practical conversation, and at my habit of putting forward every topic that admits no arduous discussion but invites serene contemplation and idle fun. But the news from England has put an end to our lotus-eating epoch, and strife found its way into George's pockets and his father's. I did not produce your most kind letter to use, lest it should increase, and renew, their anxiety. Thank God all real trouble is over now.
>
> We leave for St. Martin on Saturday, before post comes in, and I am sorry Willy is not coming here, where I should have been only too glad to welcome him . . . .[3]

After two weeks of Tegernsee, William and Helen stayed briefly in Munich, then took the train to Ried in Upper Austria. Here the Arco family owned a large estate with another vast country house. Little was thought of the border in those days. Helen wrote of the journey:-

> We had rather a grind of a journey on Saturday, what with starting at 5.10, great heat at Munich. Afterwards no room for us in the express, so that we had to 'ride the buffers,' i.e. sit on the little platform between the carriages, tremendously noisy and extremely dirty. The only alternative being the refreshment saloon which was very fusty.
>
> Then two or three hours to wait at Simbach, a dull town on the frontier, so we sat in a little inn garden and drank coffee with the village drinking beer around. Then slow trains and arriving here at 9 p.m.
>
> The villagers gave us good music during supper, a band and men's singing. It is a rather patriarchal sort of place. The brothers Arco go sometimes in the evening and drink beer with village people and the family patronise local things a good bit, but they don't seem to go and see poor people.[4]

The great house, known as Schlöss St. Martin, had a huge entrance and porch, and the roof had elaborate metal railings and onion-shaped domes around it. There was a formal garden with gravel paths, flower beds, and many stone statues. Again Helen had plenty of time to read her volumes of *Les Miserables* and write letters. She wrote to Mary at length describing their stay:-

> It's rather funny here. I don't as yet like it as much as Tegernsee. Certainly there is an absence

of my on irritation there, the constant desire, almost always thwarted, of my legs to be running about the beautiful hills, for here it is flat uninteresting country, comparatively at all events. The house is a large white one, built all round a court, something of the same sort as the ducal schlöss at Tegernsee; very difficult to find one's way about at first.

Father has a gigantic room (Lord Acton's usually) with four big windows, and a big comfortable sofa on which he likes reading French novels or other books. Windows and door wide open, too hot for draughts to hurt. I have a snug room at the other end; the only grievance that there isn't a single drawer or cupboard for clothes in it. They are all outside on the landing, so woe betide you if you want anything at a critical moment of dressing. And the bedcovers — of course I kicked off a heavy quilted thing and the huge downy thing. Then the one blanket is so small that it won't tuck so I have to fasten it to the mattress at the bottom with safety pins. I am so afraid of the maid finding out.

I'm much more sly here. There is such a pie! Besides Lord, Lady and three girls and Dick and Teeny, are Count Charles Arco, Count Max Arco, Madame something and her daughter (cousins), the tutor, the English governess, the foreign governess, and a sort of lady housekeeper, but everyone is kind.

After an enjoyable week filled with several excursions by horse and carriage it was time to start the long journey home, leaving Munich one Friday evening and arriving in London early on Sunday. The holiday, so suddenly arranged to Tegernsee and Ried had served it purpose as a change and a rest.

25
Newnham

p.s.

January 29th 1887 was a Saturday, and was thus a half-holiday for the working men of Cambridge. In the early afternoon a crowd of them, together with tradesmen who had briefly left their shops were waiting at the station for a view of Mr. Gladstone who was on his way to Sandringham. News of his visit had been made known by the local Liberal Association, resulting in a crowd forming. At what time the train would stop at Cambridge they did not know for sure, but it was understood that Mr. Gladstone was travelling with the Prince of Wales, and it could therefore be assumed that the saloon carriage would be instantly recognisable.

In due course a train going north drew into the station with a saloon carriage attached. It stopped with a sudden jolt and the crowd started to push and shout. Those who had the good fortune to be near the windows peered in pressing their faces against the glass, but where, oh where? Then the sad conclusion was passed back. This train could not be the right one. The saloon carriage contained Mr. and Mrs. Le Falbe, the Danish Ambassador, known in diplomatic circles as 'le petit Falbe,' and his wife, who had reserved it to take them from Luton to Harwich, to be sure of a restful journey. They were astonished at the cheers they received at Cambridge, but when their privacy was disturbed they showed their annoyance with disapproving gestures.

The crowd were prepared to wait, and the next train presently arrived with the saloon carriage carrying the Prince and Princess of Wales and Mr. and Mrs. Gladstone. William acknowledged the cheers and there were cries of 'speech.'

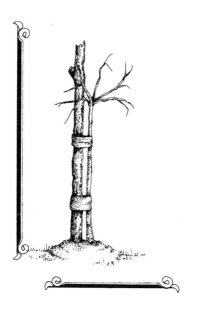

Not being entirely sure of the reception he would get at Cambridge he declined: he had already decided to make a speech when the train reached King's Lynn. The reporter from the *Cambridge Express* noticed that the Prince was amused at being ignored and was laughing to himself in the corner of the carriage.

However, the crowd were not to be disappointed, for William let it be known that he would be returning to Cambridge on Monday. It had been arranged that he and Catherine would stay with their nephew, Arthur Lyttelton, Principal of Selwyn College, for a few days. They would also visit Newnham College, where their daughter, Helen, was Vice-Principal, a post she had held since 1881.

The following Monday, 31st January, a large crowd had again gathered at Cambridge station. This time the local association of the Liberal

Party had issued a bulletin announcing that the train would arrive at 1.16 p.m., and as this happened to be during the dinner hour, a large number of people were again waiting. At the London end of the platform a barrier had been erected, forming an enclosure. Helen was standing there waiting to welcome her parents with Arthur and Kathleen Lyttelton and various members of the Liberal Party, who were packed into the enclosure. William, who wore a long military-braided and fur-lined travelling cloak was the first to alight, followed by Catherine. He was no longer Prime Minister, but what did people care about politics as the excitement increased, and the stage was set for action. He had a few words with the station master. Then, taking the arm of Helen, walked out of the enclosure towards the exit of the station, followed by Catherine, who took the arm of her nephew, Arthur Lyttelton. Everyone in the crowd tried to get a glimpse of the visitors. The scene was described in the *Cambridge Express*:-

The cheering was now continuous, and the people swarmed from off the rails, and to anywhere from whence a glimpse could be obtained of their idol. Mr. Gladstone acknowledged the applause as well as he was able under the circumstances, but one or twice it appeared as though the pressing multitude, carried away by their enthusiasm and curiosity, would precipitate the object of their devotion and worship over the edge of the platform. This was, fortunately, prevented by the ingenuity and pertinacity of the railway officials, but at the exit the crushing was frightful, and prognosticated unpleasant consequences.

It was with the utmost difficulty Mr. Gladstone was safely conducted through the narrow passage, and once the opposing force of the station master — who pushed most lustily and hustled with the determination of a practical footballer in the ex-Premier's protection — and his subordinate was removed, the crowd swept madly past like a flood through the sluice.

A young woman was severely squeezed against a wall, and men, sticks and umbrellas were discharged at tangents with curious autonomy as straws would be upon a torrent. The stream of humanity circled like a whirlpool around the open carriage, drawn by a pair of greys, that was to convey Mr. Gladstone to Selwyn.

Most of the crowd were left watching the carriage leave, but several people ran furiously to keep up with it as it drove along the streets to Selwyn College.

After lunch a visit to Newnham College had been planned where Helen worked. She was Vice-Principal, and the Principal was Nora Sidgwick, wife of Henry Sidgwick, who had done so much to set up the College. There were then two buildings: North Hall, the original building now known as Old Hall, where Helen had rooms; and South Hall, where the Sidgwicks lived, now known as Sidgwick Hall. A third hall joining the other two was in the process of being built. The women students were never allowed to go out without being escorted by a man or older woman walking with them, so part of Helen's responsibility was to ensure that they should always have a suitable person to accompany them when they went out of the College to attend lectures and laboratory demonstrations.

Bicycles were not widely used until the nineties and in any case would not have been allowed, and the girls never went on buses which were considered lowly and had sawdust on the floors. Helen was a good administrator and enjoyed advising the students and mixing with them. Unlike her father, she did not like to attract attention. Indeed Nora Sidgwick noted 'she absented herself tactfully when her family were discussed.'[1] Nora's family were influential Conservatives, and her brother, Arthur Balfour, was to become Prime Minister fifteen years later.

It must have been with a sense of relief to Helen that the visit to Newnham went according to plan. Her parents arrived with Arthur and Kathleen Lyttelton. The party were given a welcome of smiles and clapping by the students, walked round Sidgwick Hall and saw the library, and then went to Old Hall, where they stayed a little in Helen's room and talked to some of her pupils. Here Catherine to her delight and apparent astonishment was presented with a huge basket of lilies of the valley. The gift had been kept secret from Helen who was, of course, also delighted.

Then they walked to the lawn alongside the new hall being constructed under steel scaffolding to where Mr. Gladstone was to plant a plane tree. This was the highlight of the visit and the students, lecturers and other visitors, quickly encircled him to watch. Also the workmen on the new building stopped to watch and, as he appeared, started cheering:-

> The sight of the right honourable gentleman handling the spade fired the enthusiasm of a spectator, who appealed for three cheers for the Grand Old British Workman, which was responded to with much laughter and applause, to which the right honourable gentleman made answer with a smile, I shall have to take my coat off!

It was noticed that Mr. Gladstone was performing his act to the watching workmen rather than those who were directly surrounding him, but this was accepted as just as one of those things he would do, and anyway the occasion had been a success. Helen wrote to Mary:-

> He has always been so nice about Newnham, and he was very kind to such of the lecturers and students I introduced. Mama too got a much clearer and happier idea of the students — she had never been quite able to think of them as nice womanly happy girls, as they are, but dining with them and seeing in my room some I picked out, helped her to grasp the true natural state of the case much better.[2]

Helen felt thankful that the day had passed happily. The next day, Tuesday, she had persuaded her parents to attend a small party at Newnham. She described the day 'with a luncheon of Home Rulers!'

> They had an ecclesiastical breakfast at Selwyn, and later a luncheon of the best of our Home Rulers (they are rather scarce in the University). Later he submitted like a lamb to a small party at Newnham from five to six, to which I had asked about forty-five of the people who had most claim to see him . . . .

But, alas, before the party, disaster had struck, for by daylight on Tuesday morning the little tree that had been planted ceremoniously the day before had disappeared. It had been uprooted during the night and all that remained was a large hole in the ground. Helen thought it awfully funny, funny but sad. Fortunately, her infectious laughter cheered up the students when photographers, claiming to be invited by her, kept arriving to take pictures. They thought they could get a nice few orders by photographing students standing beside the new tree. Helen wrote to Mary:-

> When you see the photographs of the planting of the tree, you will notice how all the faces all around are on the broadest of grins. And here I can't help stopping to drop a tear (so to speak) on the empty grave of our poor little tree, some exceedingly trumpery blackguard having walked into the garden before daylight yesterday morning, and walked off with it bodily — a feat entirely without danger, and so the more ignoble. Distressed as we were we couldn't help roaring with laughter over the photographers, who kept arriving at different hours, summoned by notes pretending to be from me 'to photograph some of the ladies round the tree planted by Mr. Gladstone.' Two actually came with apparatus, attendants, etc. Its really very hard — we were most innocently proud and fond of our little tree, and there wasn't a creature whom it could hurt . . . . We mean to plant another in its place, but I won't have it just yet for fear the first wife will come back and find a second wife already in her place.[3]

The metaphor of the tree being likened to a wife, and a new tree to a second wife referred to the Deceased Wifes Sisters Bill. If a man's wife died (and many women died in childbirth) he was forbidden by law based on the 'table of kindred and affinity' in the Book of Common Prayer to marry her sister. The bill, introduced during William's first administration, had been passed in the Commons but thrown out in the Lords as long ago as 1871, on the grounds that a woman might be tempted to murder her sister, to get a husband. This was a great talking point.

As for the theft of the tree, the police were informed and were supplied with insulting letters that had been received by the college. Although it seemed unlikely the culprit would be caught, an undergraduate of St. John's College was accused and admitted stealing the tree, having been traced by his handwriting.[4] The tree was returned but never replanted, probably because William had planted it so firmly that the roots had been damaged when it was pulled out. Another tree was sent, an oak, and as well as receiving a letter of thanks William was sent a buttonhole of a rose-bud from the Newnham students: he liked to wear a rose-bud buttonhole in the House of Commons.

Was the tree stolen as an insult to Mr. Gladstone or to Newnham College? No doubt both were offended, and the reader will concur with his opinion that it was 'a shabby trick perpetuated by some scatterbrained or mean-spirited person upon the unoffending ladies of Newnham College.'

In July 1888 the new building was officially opened by the Princess of Wales, who with the Prince and their family attended a huge garden party to celebrate.

Had Helen, who knew the Princess quite well, used her powers of persuasion to get the royal family to come? She felt it had brought recognition to the college, for as far as the University was concerned women's colleges still did not exist. Many former students turned up, some being housed and fed for two or three days. Helen wrote to Mary:-

> I was truly thankful when it was over. I felt it was much for the social good of the college, as the Royalties coming helped to bring the Salisburys, Archbishop of Canterbury, Randolph Churchill, Lord Rosebery, Lord Acton, and various other swells.

That Helen had learnt to submit to the way women were treated is illustrated by her not feeling it worthwhile even to apply for a ticket to Charles Darwin's memorial service in Cambridge in 1882. Her family, and she in particular knew the Darwins well, who were as united a family as could be. She knew that with an address like Newnham College it was no good asking. She would not for an instant be considered.

The women students in Oxford and Cambridge did the same exams as the men and underwent the same standards of marking, but got no degrees. They could get no formal recognition from the Universities, which were willing to help the women as a set of individuals, but not their Colleges. Since its inception Newnham had suffered continuous complaints, some very far fetched: one of which for example was that students buttoned their gloves in the streets. They were expected to button them before leaving their rooms. To button gloves in the hall before going out was slovenly, but to button them in the street was worse. The legendary Miss Clough, who was Newnham's first Principal, patiently advised them how to deal with the problem:-

> I know, my dears, that you have a great deal to do and have not much time, but I don't like people to say such things about you. And so, my dears, I hope you'll get some gloves that don't want buttoning.[5]

A brilliant student was sitting in the gallery of the Senate in June 1890 between Helen and Miss Clough when it was announced that she had achieved top marks of the entire University in mathematics. The student was Philippa Fawcett. She was particularly small. She was the only child of the late Henry Fawcett, the blind Postmaster General, and of Millicent Fawcett, who had been a Miss Garret. Henry Fawcett had become blind when a young man, due to an accident when his father had let off his gun when climbing a stile, when the two were out shooting partridges. As a little girl Philippa would lead her very tall father skating on frozen ponds by singing so that he could follow her. Henry and Millicent Fawcett promoted women's suffrage; he gave women better jobs in the Post Offices, and she had been instrumental in helping Newnham College in its early stages.

When Philippa Fawcett's results were announced women students were allowed only in the gallery. As usual the men's results were read out first, and then the announcement was made: 'Women.' Philippa's mother, Millicent Fawcett, described the furore that followed:-

> The undergraduates yelled, 'Ladies,' and for some minutes there was a great uproar. A fearfully agitating moment for Philippa it must have been; the examiner, of course, could not attempt to read the names until there was a lull. Again and again he raised his cap, but would not say, 'ladies,' instead of 'women' and quite right I think. He signalled with his hand for the men to keep quiet, but he had to wait some time. At last he read Philippa's name and announced that she was above the Senior Wrangler.[6]

Newnham celebrated with a banquet, illuminations and a bonfire. Elderly Miss Clough who had returned for the occasion and was quite overcome with delight, found the festivities positively bewildering. Her faithful parlourmaid was still at the College and tried to re-assure her, saying, 'I am here,' for the parlourmaid was still the same even if a student had reached undreamed-of results.

Finally, in 1896 it seemed that degrees for women would be approved. Helen had passed her own exams at Newnham with merit and felt strongly that women students deserved recognition. In a letter to *The Times* headed 'Demand for degrees by women,' she wrote:-

> . . . . Finally, if it is still thought that the feebler brain of women must lead to the lowering of the standard of the University examinations if they are allowed to pass them, we may perhaps be permitted to give the following facts. Last year we had at Newnham 157 students, of which 49 were sent in for the tripos examinations of 1895 . . . . one fourth passed first-class and one half second-class. A remarkable feature throughout our experience of Cambridge has been the small proportion of third to second classes. This, of course, I do not mention as any indication of intellectual superiority of women to men, as doubtless the women students are, as a rule, only sent to University when they have intellectual tastes or have professional objects in view . . . .

Two weeks later, on March 13th 1896, *The Times* told of the failure of women to gain degrees in a leader:-

> The lady students at the Universities have received a cruel series of rebuffs within the last few days . . . . University of Oxford and the University of Cambridge refused to admit them to the B.A. degree . . . . Female fortitude may well be taxed by such a succession of misfortunes.

26

Golden Wedding

Earl Spencer[1] arranged to hold a reception at his own house for William and Catherine's golden wedding, and contributions were collected from close friends with a view to making a presentation gift. It was decided that portraits should be given. This all needed preparation but plans went well. William was painted by Frank Holl; Catherine by Sir Herbert Herkomer. They both looked serene and wore black, and the results were pleasing; and it was felt the portraits could be passed down to their family, which has been the case. When the donations were finally collected there was enough extra to purchase three handsome silver flower bowls. Lord Spencer must have felt it strange that there was no other event to honour the famous couple's golden wedding, but the Conservatives were in power and no doubt he was pleased that he, at least, had plans in hand. Invitations to Spencer House, St. James's, were sent out and a hundred and sixteen people accepted.

Unfortunately nobody thought to check the date. The day and month were correct; but it was a year too early. William and Catherine agreed they had better act as if it was their golden wedding day, but by the day of the reception — bad news travels quickly — everybody knew that it was a year too soon. Lord Granville, with supreme tact, was able to put a wrong to a right when making the presentation, by announcing it to be the occasion of 'entering their fiftieth year of their married life.'

As a result they were given receptions for their forty-ninth anniversary and for their fiftieth. The year between witnessed the huge Birmingham campaign, and in November Helen was allocated a few days from Newnham College to escort her parents. She afterwards claimed that the two biggest meetings her father had addressed had been in Leeds in 1881, and in Birmingham in 1888, where in Bingley Hall an estimated seventeen to eighteen thousand sat and stood. The *Birmingham Daily Gazette* reported:-

> It is almost literally correct to say that the building was crowded from floor to ceiling, for some of the galleries all around the hall reached very nearly to the roof.

Awaiting the speaker a cornet player struck up several traditional tunes. Helen noticed that the crowd were 'largely real grimy working men,' as she sat on the platform with her parents and other dignitaries, watching Mr. Osler, President of the Birmingham Liberal Association, introduce her father gesticulating with

enthusiasm. Her father had placed his top hat on the table in front of him and underneath it the papers for his speech; Mr. Osler swept his arms apart and the top hat took off with sufficient force to send the papers flying.

Mr. Gladstone spoke for one hour and fifty minutes. He grabbed a candlestick when he wanted more light. For a moment or two the candle was bobbing about in the most dangerous proximity to the speaker's chin and collar. Mrs. Gladstone looked anxious and the reporter on whose head the liquid wax was falling appeared to be growing mutinous.

Fortunately a lamp was soon provided. Helen wrote in a letter:-

Father's voice evidently carried very well. You could hear the responses sometimes from the very furthest parts; sometimes things he said would seem to strike especially the galleries on this side, on that side, or right opposite, or in the area. They were quick to catch points, and very responsive. Now and then the whole mass giving short, sharp, monosyllabic answers to a series of points.[2]

On July 25th 1889, the day the golden wedding was to be celebrated, very early in the morning a telegram was delivered from the Queen. Soon afterwards a carriage brought a letter from the Prince of Wales. Then Sir Francis Knollys called with the Prince's present, a gold inkstand. Friends who turned up soon after eight, knowing the couple to be early risers, were disappointed, finding they had gone to church. Many presents were delivered during the day. A malacca walking stick with a gold handle from Lord Rosebery; an inkstand — it was felt there could not be too many — from the former private secretaries; a breakfast service in white and gold from the Aberdeens, together with a gift that had become very popular at the time: a bracelet for Catherine with eight lockets containing a lock of her husband's hair and a lock from each member of the family: their reaction as Ishbel Aberdeen requested of each 'just a small snip,' must be left to the reader's imagination. The children themselves decided to build a porch to the house at Hawarden.

There were curious presents and touching presents. A Birmingham business man gave a pair of gold rimmed spectacles; the Southport Women's Liberal Association gave two napkin rings made of bog oak and gold edged. A deputation of workmen from Bolton arrived with a large patchwork quilt; and basket makers from Connemara sent a small basket filled with sweetly-scented asphodel, bright yellow, surrounding a photograph of themselves.

In the evening the National Liberal Club gave a party, described in the *Daily Telegraph* as 'a splendid and thoroughly enthusiastic reception.'

There were flowers everywhere, and illuminated by the miniature suns of the electric light they shone in royal profusion, clustering round columns and nestling in the fireplaces and the embrasures of the staircase. By half past eight the club was rapidly filling, and pending the arrival of the eminent visitors, the Blue Hungarian Band played in the lower smoking room, whose sacred precincts, now made glorious with forests of tiger lilies and ruby electric lamps, were for the moment invaded by many ladies, obviously curious to know what a club smoking room was like.

Mrs. Gladstone wore a black satin dress, a white fringed shawl over her shoulders, her tiara and diamond necklace, and was presented with a bouquet of yellow roses and lilies. Her husband followed leaning heavily on a stick and 'bowing and beaming to his friends on all sides.' They brought with them Stephy and Annie, Agnes and Edward, and Herbert, who watched as Viscount Oxenbridge stepped forward to make a speech and hand over firstly a golden wedding album; and, secondly, a large portrait of Mr. Gladstone and his grandson, Will[3] aged four and dressed in blue velvet with lace collar and cuffs, by Sir John Millais, 'presented by the women of England.' The reporter from the *Daily Telegraph* decided to make an estimate of the number present:-

In the library a crowd of 12,000 clustered round the ropes and barricades, and were with difficulty kept in their place by the assiduous stewards with the crimson badges . . . . A pleasant feature is the arrangement of the countless little tables that one comes across in every nook and corner, where a political or social tête à tête can be comfortably enjoyed, or an enthusiastic party made up to discuss the great events of the evening.

There was a huge display of tempting refreshments, consisting of clear soup, eight sorts of sandwiches, savoury bites of five sorts including lobster and quail, sixteen different deserts and three flavours of ices. There was champagne cup or claret cup, whisky, brandy, soda, seltzer and lemonade, followed by tea or coffee.

A few days later, on Saturday 3rd August, the G.P.s took the train from King's Cross to Queensferry. By now the children frequently referred to their parents as the G.P.s, standing for the great people, as Stephen Glynne had quietly styled them many years previously. They were accompanied by Harry and Herbert. At Queensferry Catherine opened the new railway bridge spanning the Dee between Cheshire and north Wales. It was a swinging bridge to enable big ships to pass and, at the time, was the largest in the world spanning 280 feet and having a double line of rails. Catherine turned on an electric switch to set the swinging partition in motion which was rotated by hydraulic power. She then spoke calling attention to the minority in Wales who had been so against the bridge, and to Sir Edward Watkin, a true Welshman and chairman of the Manchester, Sheffield and Lincolnshire Railway, who had promoted the erection of the bridge.

Following a luncheon party and speeches, William and Catherine, with Harry and Herbert sitting opposite, drove the two miles home in an open carriage. On entering the village they were welcomed with decorations for their golden wedding, as they had been on their wedding day; the horses were taken away and men pulled the carriage through the park. Recent months had brought sadness as well as happiness. The were pleased Harry had married Maud Rendel, the daughter of a friend of theirs in January, having suffered a broken heart in India some years previously. Yet all through the happy celebrations there was one dark cloud over them for Willy was seriously ill, and was being cared for by his affectionate wife in Devon. When Willy had had difficulty in writing his father had bought him a typewriter, but he had been unable to use it.

In September the elderly couple went to Paris, and while she rested, he went up the Eiffel Tower accompanied by Mr. Eiffel, and wrote a postcard home to Mary:-

> I never thought I should have been either wise or foolish enough to be inveigled into mounting to this height where I am writing at a comfortable table (that would dine fourteen people) under the immediate auspices of Mr. Eiffel himself. Poor Mama, who would have thoroughly enjoyed it, has not been able to come being out of sorts. The whole of this vast structure weighs only 300 tons, less I believe than a big ship. I trust all is well with you today . . .

They still both walked considerable distances , and Petz, the big black pomeranian, demanded frequent walks of his master, but more often they would use the pony cart each for the sake of the other, driving themselves or having one of the family to take the reins.

Willy died in 1891, and the old man finally retired from political life in 1894 at the age of eighty-four. The Prince and Princess of Wales twice visited Hawarden; the second time the Princess was presented with one of Petz's puppies.

The Queen, who had been so friendly during the first thirty-five years of their married life, had since 1876 been alarmed by Mr. Gladstone's political ideas which she felt were too radical. After her final farewell to the Queen, Catherine wrote:-

> The Queen sent for me to say goodbye. Naturally, my heart was full; old times rushed to my mind. All the years, the long years my husband had served Her Majesty, whilst anything done for the last time must bring so much —
>
> I was able to say what was very near my heart and which my husband is often too reticent in expressing (especially if it has report to himself). I am glad I got out what I wanted to say: that whilst everybody is liable to mistakes, one thing I could not too strongly express, his devotion to his Queen's Constitution.
>
> The Queen's answer, expressed almost with tears in her eyes, was: 'I have never doubted it.' These words pleased me; the Queen is a true woman. Nothing pleased me more (as did her whole manner so very warm and earnest) and sympathising to a great chapter. It has been a privilege this interview, and I carry away very interesting thoughts. The cordial, I may say affectionate manner towards myself, and more than all, the 'response' about my husband's devotion to the Constitution.
>
> We talked of times gone by and of her great sorrow. She, in a comforting way reminded me of the many years my husband had been given to me. Our conversation was interwoven about questions about my children: she was glad Mary had remained with me: very kind about Stephy: and Agnes's knee trouble at Lincoln: and she remarked at Stephy's marriage to his young wife and Harry's marriage, she asked about.
>
> The Queen gave me her photograph, and when the time came for the breaking up, this last visit was made very memorable, she drew me towards her and kissed me. I found it difficult to

speak and she was desolated. Our's had been a long and memorable time to look back upon, and it is only those who are going through such thoughts for *the last time* can conceive the feelings all crowding in my mind: that I was permitted to sympathise with our Queen these last fifty years — what joys and sorrows, what anxieties, and what blessings.[4]

Finally, to end on a more cheerful tone a memory of a great-nephew, from George Lyttelton, writer of the Lyttelton Hart-Davies letters, who when a small boy was punished by being locked in a room where he knocked a valuable small piece of furniture to smithereens. He was for ever grateful to his great-aunt Catherine:-

. . . . She gave me a drum, not because I had been good but, characteristically, because I had been naughty, and she thought that to punish a child of seven by locking him up in a room for several hours was wrong and stupid. The drum is no more, but Auntie Pussy has never moved from the corner which she took in my heart on that day of wrath and tears. Her great consort is not quite in that place, but he is not so very far off. And not only because he once patted me on the head.

Epilogue

In 1889 Herbert brought a case for libel: Gladstone v. Malleson, and in 1927 Herbert had a case brought against him for libel, which has since become known as 'libel against the dead,' and which was famous at the time and has been recorded in many books.

The first Court case came about when Herbert was mentioned as being co-respondent in a divorce case in an unimportant Indian paper, the *Allahbad Morning Post*. In July 1889 the London correspondent had written in his report:-

An event which would most certainly have developed into a cause célèbre has recently with great difficulty been hushed up. Of course there is a lady in the case . . . . the husband agreed to a separation from the wife without publicity. Verily Master Herbert is a chip off the old block.

Herbert would not tolerate himself and his father being slandered, especially his father, even in this little-known Indian paper. He traced the London correspondent responsible, and with his father to back him up, issued a writ in the High Court of Justice, Queen's Bench division. The case was settled with a statement from Colonel Malleson that he regretted the accusation (which he seemed to have made carelessly), and an apology was accepted in open Court.

The second case for libel involving Herbert was held in February 1927, again in the High Court of Justice. By then only two of William and Catherine's children were still alive, the youngest, Harry and Herbert. Harry was seventy-four and Herbert was seventy-three, and both lived in quiet retirement. Whilst Harry had become a prosperous businessman, Herbert had had a distinguished career which had included being Home Secretary and the first Governor-General of South Africa. He had been made a Viscount.

Their father had died in 1898 and their mother three years later. They had been married for fifty-nine years and had always been loyal and devoted to each other. Of course untrue statements are often printed in books and the press after a person is dead and, unfortunately, relations and friends cannot bring a case for libel once a person is dead. That, however, is just what Herbert wanted to do, for there had continued to be defamatory remarks about the real motivation of his father's rescue of fallen women which the family were anxious to lay to rest once and for all. Slanderous allegations against his father had long been made, but when false accusations were made in a book by Peter Wright, Herbert decided to write and tell

the author he was a liar and to make his opinion public. The author was obliged in defence of his character to issue a writ for libel, and Herbert won the case. His problem was not only to defend a person who had been dead for thirty years, but also to trace enough reliable witnesses who were still alive. The stages in which this libel case progressed now seem like fantasy.

A book, *Portraits and Criticisms*, by Captain Peter Wright was reviewed in the *Daily Mail*. The *Daily Mail* was then a more serious paper than it has become, and in the review queried whether the book would lead to a denial by the Gladstone family. In this book was printed:-

> Gladstone, who founded the great tradition since observed by many of his followers and successors with such pious fidelity, in public to speak the language of the highest and strictest principle, and in private to pursue and possess every sort of woman.

Harry and Herbert were furious. They felt that if they did not repudiate such a statement people might question why they did not speak up if it was untrue. After all, even if the book was not widely read, it was mentioned in the *Daily Mail* for all to see. The result was that Herbert wrote to the author, with a copy sent to the *Daily Mail*. His letter was explosive:-

> Mr. Peter Wright,
> Your garbage about Mr. Gladstone in *Portraits and Criticisms* has come to our knowledge. You are a liar. Because you slander a dead man, you are a coward. Because you think the public will accept invention from such as you, you are a fool.
> Gladstone
> I associate myself with this letter. H. N. Gladstone.

Captain Wright then wrote to the *Daily Mail* insisting that what was in his book was correct. The letter was published. It was on Bath Club notepaper. Both Harry and Herbert were members of the Bath Club, and to them this was an additional irritant. Herbert wrote to the Secretary complaining of Captain Wright:-

> . . . . My brother and I wrote and told him that he was a liar and a coward, the law, in the case of a dead man giving no remedy.
> In a letter published this morning by the *Daily Mail* he amplified his slander and his lies, not daring apparently to face us in Court. Again he writes on Bath Club notepaper. It seems to me that this is a matter for the Committee.
> Sincerely yours,
> Gladstone
> I have this moment received a letter from Messrs. E. Nash and Grayson, Mr. Peter Wright's publishers, to say that when they accepted the work it did not contain the passages to which we take exception. Otherwise they would have declined to publish them. It appears they were put into a proof and when it went back to the printer the publisher did not observe them.
> This shows the sort of man he is. I can tell you more about him — he is a foul fellow.

The Committee of the Bath Club decided to ask Captain Wright to resign, but when he saw the letter he demanded £100 for loss of amenities and £25 for damage to his reputation. Faced with a writ the Bath Club chose to pay up. He then took Herbert to Court for libel. This was exactly what Herbert had hoped would happen, as his solicitor had advised him it was the only method by which he could get his opinion heard in Court, but would he be able to prove that Captain Wright was a liar?

The action came before Mr. Justice Avory and a special jury in the King's Bench division of the High Court on January 27th, 1927. Mr. Boyd Merriman, K.C. appeared for Captain Wright and Mr. Norman Birkett, K.C., for Herbert. In Court Captain Wright disclosed that nearly all the people he had got his information from were dead. Although he was a young man, being half the age of the defendant, he wore a monocle and appeared supremely self-confident, for he was sure he would win his case. After much questioning from Mr. Birkett as to where he had collected his facts he exclaimed:-

'Nearly every character in history is dead. I don't know whether you have observed that Mr. Birkett.'

The trial lasted five days, and the public awaited the outcome with heightened anticipation. The front pages of the tabloid papers were taken up with photos of Harry and Herbert arriving at court wearing bowler hats and of Captain Wright wearing a trilby and his monocle. He had been educated at Harrow and Balliol College, Oxford, and was the author of several books.

On the first day Herbert was cross-examined.

'You were asked,' said Mr. Birkett, 'about your sincerity in writing the first letter in desiring a public discussion on this matter. Is it any pleasure to you to have to come into public and discuss these matters about your dead father?'

'At the age of seventy-two, as I was, to face all the muck which has been brought up by Captain Wright, and deal with it as if I was a scavenger? Do you think it was a pleasant duty?'

Mr. Birkett: 'Did the prospect of having to come into court and discuss the memory of your father and hear these things said afford you any pleasure?'

'No, but we had to do it because we knew — my brother and I — that when we passed away this Captain Wright might perhaps in a further publication have said: there were two sons of Mr. Gladstone living when I made these statements and they dared not take any notice.'

Herbert then gave the names of a number of institutions for the rescue of fallen women with which Mr. Gladstone was associated, and other bodies for carrying out social work.

Mr. Birkett: 'Do you know whether your father spoke to such women in the street?'

Herbert replied: 'Yes. I did not happen to see him, but I know he did.'

The next day Captain Wright was in the witness box. Amongst his statements two caught the attention of the public. There seemed to be no doubt in his mind that he was correct, or so it seemed.

Captain Wright recorded that he had once seen a man called Cecil Gladstone in Eastbourne; he resembled the P.M. and was his illegitimate son. Actually Cecil was the son of his cousin, another William Gladstone. Well prepared, Mr. Birkett produced a birth certificate and *Lodge's Peerage*, which were handed up to the witness, who apologised for his mistake. Although Cecil was no longer alive, his wife later arrived and caused a stir in the Court.

Everybody knew the reputation of Lily Langtry when Captain Wright mentioned suggestive innuendos in her relationship with Mr. Gladstone.

Mr. Birkett questioned Captain Wright: 'Mrs. Langtry is alive, is she not?'

'Yes, she lives on the Riviera.'

'Do you think some of the answers you have given in the witness box might cause grievous pain to her?'

'I am afraid so. It very much annoys me that it should be so. I am very sorry about it — more than I can say. I would have done anything I could to avoid it.'

The judge interspersed: 'You don't like reflecting on a living person?'

Captain Wright: 'Not a woman.'

Again Mr. Birkett was well prepared. He held up a telegram before reading it out: 'Strongly repudiate slanderous accusations by Peter Wright. Lily Langtry.'

Finally after ten hours in the witness box Captain Wright said of what he had written:

'I do not regret it because it is untrue, but because it caused pain to Mr. Gladstone's family. I would still express regret if they would retract their statement that I am a liar, a coward, and a fool. I regret that I hurt their feelings.'

Again pressed by Mr. Birkett's questioning Captain Wright hit the witness box with a resonance that echoed through the hushed Court as he emphasised each word:

'I regret most emphatically hurting the feelings of Lord Gladstone and his family, and if they had given me anything of a chance I would have said so. I would say so now.'

'Don't knock the furniture about,' said the judge.

The jury were out for two and a half hours and entered the Court at a quarter past seven on February 3rd.

Mr. Justice Avory: 'I understand you are all agreed that the gist of the letter of Lord Gladstone on July 27th was true?'

To this the foreman of the jury replied yes, and amidst the increasing noise in the Court he could just be heard to say:

'I would like to add that it is the unanimous opinion of the jury that the evidence that has been placed before them completely vindicates the high moral character of the late Mr. W. E. Gladstone.'

In the gallery the people began to stamp their feet until the judge brought instant silence with a stern threat that the next demonstrator would be committed for contempt of court. Immediately the trial was over Captain Wright made an unqualified apology in a letter to Herbert, and sent a copy to the *Daily Mail*.

Sources

Quotations from Mary Gladstone's diaries are taken from *Mary Gladstone, her diaries and letters*, edited by Lucy Masterman, 1930. Quotations from Lucy Cavendish's diaries are from *The Diary of Lady Frederick Cavendish*, edited by John Bailey, 1927.

BL = The British Library Reference Division, Department of Manuscripts.
CRO = Clwyd Record Office, Hawarden, Deeside, Clwyd.

Introduction
1. BL 46220.
2. BL 46219.

Chapter 1.
1. *Early Public Life of William Ewart Gladstone*, by A. F. Robbins, (undated).
2. *Contributions towards a Glossary of the Glynne Language* by a Student (George Lyttelton) 1904.

Chapter 2.
1. CRO Box 22/4.
2. CRO Box 22/4.
3. BL 46269.
4. CRO Box 22/4.
5. BL 44370(35).
6. CRO Box 22/6.
7. CRO Box 22/6.

Chapter 3.
1. Nora, daughter of Henry and Lavinia Glynne.
2. BL 46219(2) edited.
3. Diary of 1860 of Agnes Gladstone.

Chapter 4.
1. *Pages from the Diary of an Oxford Lady 1843—62*, by Margaret Jane Gifford, (undated).
2. BL Loan 73.
3. BL Loan 73.
4. *Letters of the Prince Consort 1831—61*, selected and edited by Dr. Kurt Jagow.
5. BL 46219(4).

6. Edward Cardwell, M.P.
7. BL 46219(4).
8. BL 46219(96)
9. *Letters of Queen Victoria*, second series, edited by Dr. A. C. Benson and Viscount Esher, 1926.
10. BL 44252(1).
11. BL 46219(20).
12. BL 46219(21) edited.

Chapter 5.
1. CRO Box 22/6.
2. Later first Duke of Westminster.

Chapter 6.
1. Colonel Fenwick, London Hospital meeting. CRO Box 128.
2. *Portrait of the Seventies*, by G. W. E. Russell, 1885.
See *The London*, by A. E. Clark-Kennedy, 1963; and *King Cholera*, by Norman Longmate, 1966.

Chapter 7.
1. CRO Box 124E/7.
2. *The Times*, September 27, 1870.
3. *Annals of an Eton House*, by Ernest Gambier Parry, 1907.

Chapter 8.
1. *Life and Letters*, by Dorothy Neville, 1898.
2. *Years of Content*, by G. Leveson-Gower, 1940.
3. BL 46228(42).
4. *For My Grandchildren*, by H.R.H. Princess Alice, Countess of Athlone, 1965.

Chapter 9.
1. See *Woman and Philanthropy in Nineteenth Century England*, by K. F. Prochaska, 1980.
2. CRO Box 128/6.
3. *Catherine Gladstone*, by Edwin A. Pratt, 1898.

Chapter 10.
1. BL Loan 73.
2. *The Times*, June 2, 1875.
3. Sold at Christies, June 27, 1875, for £483; £94 10s; £105; £53 11s, respectively. See *The Times*.
4. *The Times*, June 28, 1875.
5. BL 46220(31).
6. *More Leaves from the Journal of a Life in the Highlands* (1862—82), by H.M. Queen Victoria, 1884.
7. *Victorian Duke*, by Gervase Huxley, 1983.
8. BL 46220(35).
9. BL 46220(37).
10. Sir Thomas Gladstone's daughter.
11. *The Queen*, March 26, 1871.

Chapter 11.
1. Dated April 14, 1873. BL Loan 73.
2. *The Wedgwoods: being a life of Josiah Wedgwood*, by Llewellyn Jewitt, 1865.
3. *For My Grandchildren*, by H.R.H. Princess Alice, Countess of Athlone, 1965.
4. CRO Box 42/4.
5. BL Loan 73.
6. BL Loan 73.
7. BL Loan 73.
8. BL Loan 73 (copy letter).

Chapter 12.
1. CRO Box 40.
2. CRO Add. 28/45 edited.
3. *The Life of William Ewart Gladstone*, edited by Sir Wemyss Reid, 1899. (See page 604.)

Chapter 13.
1. *Daily Telegraph*, June 19, 1874.
2. *Chester Chronicle*, August 3, 1872.
3. *Chester Chronicle*, August 10, 1872.
4. Glynne of Hawarden Family Papers and Documents, National Library of Wales, Aberystwyth, Dyfed.

Chapter 14.
1. BL 46235(36).
2. *South London Chronicle*, March 5, 1870.
3. CRO Box 23/2.
4. *The Times*, December 30, 1873.

5. CRO Box 42/4.
6. *George Douglas, Eighth Duke of Argyle, Autobiography & Memoirs*, 1906.
7. *The Times*, October 1, 1875.

Chapter 15.
1. BL 46271.
2. *A Lady's Maid in Downing Street*, by Auguste Schlüter, 1922.
3. *Thirteen Years in a Busy Woman's Life*, by Mrs. Alec Tweedie, 1912.
4. *A Lady's Maid in Downing Street*, by Auguste Schlüter, 1922.

Chapter 16.
1. BL 46320.
2. BL 46271.
3. *Reynold's Newspaper*, December 10, 1893.
4. *Reynold's Newspaper*, December 17, 1893.
5. *Liverpool Daily Post*, December 19, 1893.

Chapter 17.
1. *Some Hawarden Letters, 1878— 1913, written to Mrs. Drew*, edited by Lisle March-Phillipps and Bertram Christian, 1917.

Chapter 18.
1. Worcester Herald, March 20, 1880.

Chapter 19.
1. *Reminiscences*, by Lord Kilbracken, 1931.
2. *Years of Content*, by G. Leveson-Gower, 1905.
3. *The Diary of Sir Edward Walter Hamilton, K. C.B., 1880— 85*, edited by Dudley W. R. Bahlman, 1972.
4. BL 46219(116)
5. BL 46219(118)

Chapter 20.
1. CRO Box 40.

Chapter 21.
1. *The Morning Post*, September 3, 1883.
2. *The Private Life of Queen Alexandra*, by Hans Roger Madol, 1940.
3. Ibid.
4. Laura Tennant's diary.
5. *The Morning Post*, September 18, 1883.
6. *After Thirty Years*, by Viscount (Herbert) Gladstone, 1928.

Chapter 22.
1. BL 46228(244).
2. *Pall Mall Gazette*, August 1, 1885.
3. *Years of Content*, by G. Leveson-Gower, 1905.
4. *The Morning Post*, August 10, 1885.
5. BL 46226(58) edited.
6. *Sunbeam R.Y.S.*, by Earl Brassey, G.C.B., D.C.L., 1927.
7. BL 46226(58) edited.

Chapter 23.
1. *Mary Ponsonby*, by Magdalen Ponsonby, 1927.
2. Duke of Westminster, formerly Marquis of Westminster who, as Earl Grosvenor, was M.P. for Chester.
3. BL 46229(5).

Chapter 24.
1. CRO Box 40.
2. BL 46231(82).
3. BL 46228(140).
4. BL 46231(89).

Chapter 25.
1. *Mrs. Henry Sidgwick*, by Ethel Sidgwick, her niece, 1938.
2. CRO Box 40.
3. CRO Box 44/3.
4. *Cambridge Express*, February 23, 1887.
5. *Memoirs of Anne Jemima Clough*, by B. A. Clough, 1897.
6. *What I remember*, by M. G. Fawcett, 1924

Chapter 26.
1. Fifth Earl of Spencer.
2. BL 46231(98).
3. William Glynne Charles Gladstone (1885—1915) only son of Willy and Gerty, became an M.P. Killed in action.
4. BL 46219(70) edited.
5. St. Deiniol's memorial lecture, by Hon. G. W. Lyttelton, published privately 1955.

FAMILY TREE

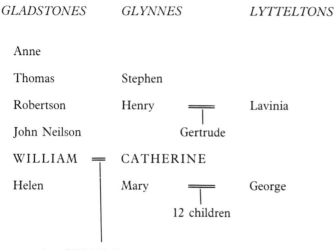

GLADSTONES   *GLYNNES*   *LYTTELTONS*

Anne

Thomas   Stephen

Robertson   Henry   ═══   Lavinia

John Neilson   Gertrude

WILLIAM ═ CATHERINE

Helen   Mary   ═══   George

                         12 children

   1.   WILLY (b. 3.6.1840)
   2.   AGNES (b. 18.10.1842)
   3.   STEPHY (b. 4.4.1844)
   4.   JESSY (b. 27.7.1845: d.1850)
   5.   MARY (b. 23.11.1847), also called Maizie
   6.   HELEN (b. 28.8.1849), also called Lena
   7.   HARRY (b. 2.4.1852), also called Henry
   8.   HERBERT (b. 7.1.1854)